ON LIFE'S JOURNEY
ALWAYS BECOMING

For Garey,

with deep gratitude,

Dan Lindley

Evanston

March 2011

For Lucia Woods

We shall not cease from exploration
And the end of all our exploring
Will be to arrive where we started
And know the place for the first time.
                                   —T. S. Eliot

Still crazy after all these years.
                        —Simon and Garfunkel

ON LIFE'S JOURNEY

ALWAYS BECOMING

DANIEL A. LINDLEY

CHIRON PUBLICATIONS

WILMETTE, ILLINOIS

All photographs are by the author.
The photograph on page 41 was arranged and composed by Lucia Woods

LIBRARY OF CONGRESS CATALOGING-IN-PUBLICATION DATA

Lindley, Daniel A.
  On life's journey : always becoming / Daniel A. Lindley.
  p. cm.
  Includes bibliographical references and index.
  ISBN 1-888602-40-6 (hardcover : alk. paper) —
  ISBN 1-888602-36-8 (pbk. : alk. paper)
  1. Individuation (Psychology) 2. Archetype (Psychology) 3.
Jungian psychology. 4. Individuation (Psychology) in literature.
I. Title.
  BF175.5.I53L56 2006
  155.2'5—dc22

                                                          2006010466

          Hardcover EAN: 978-1-888602-40-1
          Paperback EAN: 978-1-888602-36-4

CONTENTS

PREFACE

THIS BOOK IS a reflection on our life's journey, from birth to old age. I use art, notably poems, as examples of ordered portrayals of that journey, throughout. My own life and, in a more limited way, the lives of three people close to me, flesh out (literally) my argument. C. G. Jung's theory of archetypes underlies the whole. Let me amplify each of these in turn.

First, poetry. In a former life, before I became an analyst, I was a teacher and professor of English. I am well aware, from having taught junior and senior high school English for nine years, that poetry is strange stuff for most people. But I do not depend on my reader's prior knowledge of how to read poems. Rather, I offer poetry as tracings of thoughts and feelings that all of us have had. Helen Vendler, in the introduction to her marvelous text *Poems, Poets, Poetry*, writes: "Chapter One, 'The Poem as Life,' uses several short poems to show how a poetic utterance springs from a life-moment..." (1997, p. v). That is exactly my reason for including poems. Think of the poet telling you something, sharing something that happened, either in the world or within the heart—or both. The poet speaks, revealingly. All you need do is listen attentively. Try to imagine what that "life moment" would have been like if it had happened to you.

Next, the use of my own life's history and the lives of three others who have been, at different times and in different ways, at the center of my story. I write more extensively of my infancy and childhood because that is the most open time of life, before consciousness (that is, self-consciousness) gets in the way. The three other people are women in my memory and in my life. I write about my own history because I feel it is all I can really know, but my hope (and belief) is that some of it will resonate with yours. Introverts, and I am one, know themselves first. Extroverts know others first. An extrovert writing this book would people it, I imagine, with a wide range of examples, which I do not have. My gratitude to those people I do include goes far beyond any telling of it that I might manage.

Then, the underlying Jungian theory of archetypes. The concept of the archetype, the idea of individuation, the importance of dreams, the reconciliation of opposites through the "transcendent function"— all these are part and parcel of this book, and they are all Jungian. But I have seldom referenced the Jungian sources. My aim here is to provide a description of individuation based on what happens in particular lives. Referencing of sources changes the focus from particulars to theory, to "knowledge" or "understanding." Good things, too, but such writing in the service of understanding has been done superbly by many others in the Jungian world: I enthusiastically commend to my reader Edward Edinger, *Ego and Archetype* (1972); June Singer, *Boundaries of the Soul* (1994); Murray Stein, *Jung's Map of the Soul* (1998), and Edward Whitmont, *The Symbolic Quest* (1969). Jung himself wrote eighteen volumes (and then some) about a universe of subjects, a fact which is as daunting as his prose style. But it is all there, in his *Collected Works*.

So this book has a personal story, together with poems, with a theory of archetypes to inform them. Expect a more personal voice with the story and the poems, and a somewhat more theoretical voice when I come to deal with life's stages and their connections with the archetypal ground. I try to show how experience negotiates with theory, and theory with experience. Ultimately they are inseparable. Jung, supplying part of my title, puts forth theory but combines it with feelings:

In every adult there lurks a child—an eternal child, something that is always becoming, is never completed, and calls for unceasing care, attention, and education. That is the part of the human personality that wants to develop and become whole. (1954, 169–170)

The theoretical archetypal child in us is the same as any actual child: both need "unceasing care, attention, and education," and both want to develop.

What is the importance of reflecting on the journey of our life? Socrates famously observed that the unexamined life is not worth living. That is surely so, but I believe that there is a deeper and more compelling reason to live an examined life. It is this: the unexamined life is fundamentally *unethical*. In *Memories, Dreams, Reflections*, Jung explains,

I took great care to try to understand every single image, every item of my psychic inventory... and, above all, to realize them in actual life.... Insight into them must be converted into an ethical obligation. Not to do so is to fall prey to the power principle, and this produces dangerous effects which are destructive not only to others but even to the knower. The images of the unconscious place a great responsibility upon a man [sic]. Failure to understand them, or a shirking of ethical responsibility, deprives him of his wholeness and imposes a painful fragmentariness on his life. (1973, 192–193)

Because my subject is the individual psyche through the course of life, I have little to say about the larger society, the collective. But the collective, "the people," is not one creature. It is made up of individuals. In these times it is all too easy to lose sight of an individual's life. The "dangerous effects" Jung refers to are all too present when the political life of a country becomes polarized, as it is in the United States as I write these words. Both the right and the left, because they confuse worldly power with "truth," neglect the inner life.

First, the political right. James Moffett, writing in the context of a textbook-banning controversy, described a number of right-wing organizations, such as the Heritage Foundation and the Moral Majority, thus:

> What links them across differences in style and decorum is, contrary to all New Right rhetoric, a profound lack of faith, a negative conviction about human beings, a fear of individual development, and an authoritarian reliance on a sort of group mind. The positive, free-spirited individualism claimed by the New Right represents an attempt to overcome this negativism by denying it and by fantasizing its opposite. The fact is... that planks in the platform of this reactionary conservatism correspond to symptoms in the syndrome of agnosis [fear of knowledge], which in the wake of Hitlerism many psychologists studied extensively as the "authoritarian" or "prefascist" or "dogmatic" personality. A salient trait, they determined, is the rejection of self-examination in favor of crusading against evils one unconsciously wants to eradicate from one's self. (1988, 193)

Self-examination is, as Jung said, an ethical obligation. Self-examination always means coming upon guilt and darkness. As Moffett says, many people fear finding such darkness within, so they seek security in certainties outside themselves.

But there is equal authoritarianism, and an equal search for certainties, on the left. Environmental activism can lead to identification with the savior archetype, just as religious fundamentalism can. There is always inflation, unjustified pride, in "knowing" what is right, whether it is saving the spotted owl or preserving the wetlands. Self-knowledge is not a cause, or a conviction about what the outer world ought to be. Rather, it flows from reflection, which yields a continual awareness of the light and the shadow in our lives. Awareness nourishes humility. We can humbly reflect upon what we can know of our life's journey.

And we do have some knowledge. The path we walk is not unknown; it has purpose and direction. We are living out stories that have been there long before us and will be there long after we are gone. We are separate and together at once. Our separateness is derived from the accidents and circumstances of our particular lives, but our common ground is the archetypal ground. To lose sight of that common ground, or (worse) never to have been aware of it, is to be dangerously overcommitted to an unreflective life lived in accordance only with incomplete and seductively simple "truths." Our ethical obligation is to reflect, in bright times and dark, on our journey. Quiet reflection makes the world seem more complicated, but out of that complexity patterns emerge. This book is about those patterns.

ACKNOWLEDGMENTS

THERE ARE PEOPLE not otherwise in this book to whom I owe much: other family, mentors, patients, colleagues and friends who have been with me. My mother and father *are* in the book, but here I want to thank them for this curious fact: Not a word about an inner life was to be heard from either of them. Even though it must have been clear very early on that I was living in a quieter, more private world than they did, they never made me feel odd; indeed, their silence about the inner world made it the more tantalizing for me. My son and daughter are constant sources of energy and bringers of news of the world-as-it-is. Their children, just by being children, inform me. Teachers: Cleanth Brooks, who taught me how poetry works, and James McCrimmon, who introduced me to rhetorical theory. William Rogge, who taught me about teaching itself. Ray Johnson, Egyptologist, art historian, and friend, who read an early draft, helped with details from his specialty, and brought to his reading the ancient Egyptians' ideas about life, time, and death, along with his own. In the Jungian world, Murray Stein and Nathan Schwartz-Salant, for their support of this book; my analysts, Garey Malek and Anne Avery, and my supervisor, Peter Mudd. Liliane Frey-Rohn, for an evening in Zurich that she made into one of the most extraordinary instances of being seen that my wife and I have ever had. Fellow candidates all, finding our way through Jungian thought and, with fear and delight, through ourselves. Patients and supervisors at the North Chicago VA Medical Center, and at Rush-Presbyterian Hospital, where I trained; and, finally, my own patients over these twenty years, some of whom had to be willing to trust a person just starting. They shared their lives with me. Here I hope to return the favor they have done me, at least a little.

I am grateful for permission to quote, as noted, from the following:

Beckett, Samuel. From *Waiting For Godot* by Samuel Beckett. Reprinted by permission of Grove/Atlantic, Inc.

Eliot, T. S. From "The *Boston Evening Transcript*" by T. S. Eliot. © The T. S. Eliot Estate. Reprinted by permission of the publisher, Faber and Faber Ltd.

Eliot, T. S. From "East Coker" and "The Dry Salvages" from *Four Quartets*, © 1942 by T. S. Eliot and renewed 1970 by Esme Valerie Eliot. Reprinted by permission of Harcourt, Inc., and Faber and Faber Ltd.

Eliot, T. S. Excerpt from *The Family Reunion: A Play*, © 1939 by T. S. Eliot and renewed 1967 by Esme Valerie Eliot, reprinted by permission of Harcourt Brace & Company and Faber and Faber Ltd.

Eliot, T. S. From "Little Gidding" from *Four Quartets*, © 1942 by T. S. Eliot and renewed 1970 by Esme Valerie Eliot. Reprinted by permission of Harcourt, Inc., and Faber and Faber Ltd.

Eliot, T. S. From "The Love Song of J. Alfred Prufrock" by T. S. Eliot. © The T. S. Eliot Estate. Reprinted by permission of the publisher, Faber and Faber Ltd.

Ferlinghetti, Lawrence. From *A Coney Island of the Mind* by Lawrence Ferlinghetti, © 1958 by Lawrence Ferlinghetti. Reprinted by permission of New Directions Publishing Corp.

Frost, Robert. Excerpt from "Desert Places" from *The Poetry of Robert Frost,* edited by Edward Connery Lathem. Copyright 1936 by Robert Frost, © 1964 by Lesley Frost Ballantine, © 1969 by Henry Holt and Company. Reprinted by permission of Henry Holt and Company, LLC.

Hall, Donald. "The Sleeping Giant" from *Old and New Poems* by Donald Hall, © 1990 by Donald Hall. Reprinted by permission of Houghton Mifflin Company. All rights reserved.

Jung, C. G. From Jung, C. G.; *The Practice of Psychotherapy,* © 1966 Bollingen, renewed 1994. Reprinted by permission of Princeton University Press.

CHAPTER 1

THE ARCHETYPAL GROUND
A TREASURABLE VISION

THE SUBJECT OF this book is the archetypal ground that underlies our journey from birth to death. That ground is universal,
ever-present, and experienced as image and feeling. Because William
Wordsworth's great poem "Ode: Intimations of Immortality from
Recollections of Early Childhood" has the same subject, I refer to it
throughout. In it, he wrote:

> ... those first affections,
> Those shadowy recollections,
> Which, be they what they may,
> Are yet the fountain-light of all our day,
> Are yet a master-light of all our seeing;
> Uphold us, cherish, and have power to make
> Our noisy years seem moments in the being
> Of the eternal silence: truths that wake,
> To perish never....
>
> (1948, 232)

This book is about the "shadowy recollections" that will inform
our life at any moment when we are open to them. Wordsworth, in
his famous ode, remembers openness as the essence of childhood,
and he goes on to describe its loss as we grow older. There is high
drama in Wordsworth's creation of the poem out of the materials of
his own examined life. It begins with a vivid description of how fresh
and marvelous the world had once seemed, a joy followed by pain
and loss because that primal delight in things had "fled."

Wordsworth lost his mother when he was eight, and his father five years later. His life was by turns calm and adventurous. The French Revolution, with which he was passionately involved, was an enormous outer instance of the expansion of sensibility we now call the Romantic Movement. Wordsworth faced monumental questions and left us with a body of poetry much of which is an affirmation of universal ideas, insights, contained in very particular experiences. Such particulars were not, previously, the stuff of which Western art was supposed to be made. Art had been thought to flourish exclusively within an aristocracy of class and education. One has only to read Pope's *Essay on Man* to hear aristocratic philosophical abstraction, rather than introspection, at work: "Heav'n from all creatures hides the book of Fate, / All but the page prescrib'd, their present state;..." (1969, 124). Wordsworth seldom generalizes about "all creatures," and the idea of a "book of Fate" would not be congenial to him. For example, Wordsworth's *Prelude* documents the growth of his own, particular awareness: its full title is, *The Prelude or, Growth of a Poet's Mind/An Autobiographical Poem.* "Fair seed-time had my soul," Wordsworth wrote at the beginning of this poem, "and I grew up/Fostered alike by beauty and by fear...." Here is his portrayal of one sort of a childhood fear:

> For many days, my brain
> Worked with a dim and undetermined sense
> Of unknown modes of being; o'er my thoughts
> There hung a darkness, call it solitude
> Or blank desertion. No familiar shapes
> Remained, no pleasant images of trees,
> Of sea and sky, no colors of green fields;
> But huge and mighty forms, that do not live
> Like living men, moved slowly through the mind
> By day, and were a trouble to my dreams.
>
> (1948, 244)

We will encounter another "huge and mighty" form—a sleeping giant—in our discussion of childhood. But here, listen to the fear of abandonment, and the concomitant fear of a world populated by forms unknown. Pope's abstractions embody no such memories. Pope starts with a general proposition: we can only know our present state. Wordsworth enters that state and gives us its details, its feelings, its life. Archetypes only matter when they are experienced concretely.

Of the "Intimations" ode, Wordsworth wrote:

> To that dream-like vividness and splendour which invests objects of sight in childhood, every one, I believe, if he would look back, could bear testimony,... but having in the poem regarded it as presumptive evidence of a prior state of existence, I think it right to protest against a conclusion ... that I meant to inculcate such a belief. It is far too shadowy a notion to be recommended to faith, as more than an element in our instincts of immortality.... Having to wield some of its elements when I was impelled to write this poem on the Immortality of the Soul, I took hold of the notion of pre-existence as having sufficient foundation in humanity for authorizing me to make for my purpose the best use of it I could as a poet. (1948, 1118)

Wordsworth, in short, is working with an idea—"instincts of immortality"—that has, as he says, "sufficient foundation in humanity." His task in the poem is to make that idea into concrete experience by giving us examples. That is my strategy also. I, like Wordsworth, depend upon a theory of pre-existence that applies universally. Not of the soul; I do not presume to take on that question. The pre-existent structure I depend on is the archetype-several in particular, and, more generally, the presence, under all our experience, of an archetypal ground which is permanent, unchanging, and, above all, there. (I will get to "where" below.) I am convinced that the archetypes have "sufficient foundation in humanity." Let me amplify, therefore, what it means to conceive of archetypes, and of an archetypal ground.

Imagine the moment of beginning to read a story or a poem. Or remember the feeling in the theater as the house lights dim but the curtain has not yet risen. Or the moment just before entering an exhibition of Rembrandt etchings or Egyptian Old Kingdom sculpture. Or the moment after the orchestra has become silent, as we await the conductor's first gesture and the first coruscation of sound. In each of these situations we are expectant and, to some degree at least, trusting. We trust that we will shortly experience something more ordered than our commonplace world. Literature, painting, sculpture and music differ from daily life because they are *shaped*. They have explicit or implicit *plots*. Their worlds are not governed by accident or caprice. Rather, they are governed by form. Form makes meaning by keeping meaninglessness—in other words, chaos—at bay. That is one reason why art matters. Art differs from daily life because daily life "just happens." But suppose we were to discover form in our ordinary experience—form of the sort we find in art, story, or music. We would then have a new view of ourselves: a view that says we are living a story that has a structure, indeed a structure that we can know. The argument of this book is that our lives *are* structured, shaped by forces emanating from the common ground of the archetypes. Knowing the structure can defeat helplessness by giving meaning to the course of our life.

The underlying structure is hard for us to see, though. As T. S. Eliot observed, we are "distracted from distraction by distraction" (1943, 6). Our lives are so cluttered, so full of demands, so fast-paced, that we lose sight of the ordering forces underneath daily life. This is a great loss indeed. That loss of a sense of shape, of form, of plot—of art in life, if you will—may lead us to feel that life is capriciously unpredictable, which in turn gives rise to the feeling that we are powerless to change things. This feeling is summed up, frighteningly, in *King Lear* by the just-blinded and deceived Gloucester: "As flies are to wanton boys, we are to the Gods: they kill us for their sport" (1986, IV, 1). For Samuel Beckett even a moment of affirmation may be immediately undermined, as in *Waiting for Godot*. There, the two tramps have been waiting, and Godot has not appeared:

Vladimir: We are not saints, but at least we have kept our appointment. How many others can boast as much?
Estragon: Billions. (1976, II)

Vladimir argues that each of us is unique. Estragon posits a mass of billions of people, all of them waiting. Estragon's view resonates with our times of waiting for an end to feelings of emptiness and lack of meaning. We wait, burdened by the conviction that no one could escape from whatever dark place we have come to in our life.

Art is no escape from darkness or chaos, but it presents us with such states in settings where we know they are coming, and where we know there will be a resolution, an understanding, a clarification. The dark moments in tragedy are balanced, at the end, by moments of transcendent vision. For example, King Lear, having at last come to an understanding of his horrifyingly inflated sense of himself, imagines life anew with his now-loved daughter. They are imprisoned, and yet he says, "[We'll] take upon 's the mystery of things / As if we were God's spies" (1986, V, 1). It is a treasurable vision, and we shall return to it. The fact that such a vision always comes too late in tragedy does not mitigate its value: we can read or see the play again and again, and keep reliving its vision for ourselves. Another example: Heracles, at the end of Sophocles' *The Women of Trachis,* is caught in the incinerating shirt of Nessus that is burning away his flesh. One might expect him to despair, or to be enraged. But, instead, he cries out, in Ezra Pound's version, *"SPLENDOUR! IT ALL COHERES!"* (2003, 1108).

Or consider this: a series of Rembrandt self-portraits shows us not only the advance of age and decrepitude but also the unflinching courage and objectivity of the artist as he minutely records the accretions of age, of life itself, on his face. In a world in flux and full of false appearances, art is permanence that contains the truths of despair and triumph. Each time we reread a play, a poem, or a novel, or look again at a painting, we return to the same conflicted, multi-faceted, but known world. Art stays. It is we who change.

It is because of this "staying," this permanence, that the examples in this book are drawn largely from literature. But we live *with* litera-ture, not in it. To represent the opposite of literature's unchanging-ness I use some particulars from my own life's journey. I know them, and have reflected on their meanings, insofar as I can. Life and lit-erature illuminate one another: an interpretation of a poem is also an autobiographical document. I make use of the space where literature and experience overlap, the space where the permanent and the tran-sitory merge, at least momentarily. I am not doing literary criticism or scholarship; I simply use literature as if it were actual experience.

Now, a way of looking at all of this. Two pairs of opposites govern how we see ourselves and the world. Our view of the world (at any given moment) may be located on this continuum:

ORDER . . . . CHAOS

And our view of ourself at any given moment may be located on this one:

HERO/HEROINE . . . . VICTIM

Not only may we locate ourselves and our sense of our world; we may also do the same thing with our examples from literature. Thus, King Lear at the beginning of the play is convinced that he deter-mines the order of things. He believes he lives on the far left of both polarities. He not only sees his world as orderly, he also sees himself as the source of that order. His daughters Regan and Goneril, driven by selfish, worldly ambitions, can only mirror his idea of order back to him, but his daughter Cordelia, because she has her own inner idea of order, does not; and it is King Lear's reaction to all of this that gets the plot underway. As the play proceeds, the king experiences chaos in the world—in a raging storm—and in himself: his madness. Just before his death, as we have seen, he achieves a new view of the world that has the potential of seeing everything—hero and victim, order and chaos. Speaking to Cordelia, he says:

[S]o we'll live,
And pray, and sing, and tell old tales, and laugh....
And take upon 's the mystery of things
As if we were God's spies;... (1986. v, 3)

It is a vision that unifies the opposites of *things,* on the one hand, and *mystery,* on the other. Such a vision is a lifetime's achievement, as we shall see. For King Lear, it is a vision made possible by the fact that he no longer has any power, any kingship: he and Cordelia are in prison. Power, kingship, arbitrary control, have been his whole life until this moment. Only after he has had his whole previous life taken from him can he really see how the world looks, and see his true place in it. Only in prison does he gain, finally and wonderfully, the freedom to see with what Wordsworth calls "the philosophic mind" (1948,234). Philosophy is here used in its larger sense, of love of insight, knowledge and understanding, with all their concomitant humilities.

Infants experience these same opposites: feelings of illusory power followed by life-threatening abandonment. An infant lives at the extremes. Hungry and crying, an infant is victim in an indifferent and therefore seemingly chaotic world. Being fed, that same infant, having "caused" the breast to appear, is an omnipotent god or goddess in a world that, because it (for now) supplies everything, seems perfectly ordered. The growing child also has times of heroism and times of victimhood, and the distance between these states increases exponentially in adolescence. The young adult still feels the tension of the two but tries to avoid victimhood and find some measure of the heroic in thought or deed or both. Age can bring the view that includes everything, but of course it may not. These stages are the subjects of the chapters of this book.

Anyone familiar with stage theory will recognize Erik Erickson here, and Jung, and Joseph Campbell's hero myth. I am not adding to that literature. Rather, my topic is the underlying pattern that informs each stage. That pattern emerges most clearly as a series of *activated archetypes*. As we move through life we enter, one after another, the force fields of particular archetypes. It is necessary at the beginning, therefore, to have an idea of the concept of the archetype.

Suppose we decide to try to live out King Lear's wish, to take upon ourselves the mystery of things. To do this would be to try for the deepest and most subtle vision of why things happen. Today the search for answers to the big "why" questions is conducted by scientists, philosophers, theologians—not most of the rest of us. Nevertheless, King Lear's wish would require of us the longest perspective we can achieve.

At the end of the first act of Thornton Wilder's play *Our Town* (Wilder's humble setting for embodying great questions), George and his little sister Rebecca are talking as they look out of an upstairs window at the moon and the night sky. The sky and the stars remind Rebecca of a letter written to a friend, Jane Crofut, by her minister when Jane was sick. The minister addressed the letter in the usual way, to Jane Crofut, The Crofut Farm, Grover's Corners, New Hampshire. George does not see anything unusual about that, and impatiently says so, but Rebecca then tells him that the address went on: Grover's Corners, New Hampshire, The United States of America, The Western Hemisphere, The Earth, The Solar System, The Universe and, finally, The Mind of God. George is impressed. And then Rebecca informs George that the postman brought the letter anyway! This fact impresses George even more. George and Rebecca stay at the window, looking at the stars, but the story of the letter's address has reminded them, and all of us, as audience, of where we are in relation to much larger presences. Those larger presences may be understood as the archetypes, but "understood" is too narrow a word. George and Rebecca are reminded, by the address on the envelope, of what is beyond them, and their feeling of awe is palpable as they gaze up at the night sky. All of us have felt this. It is a feeling beyond "understanding," engendered as it is by the presence of the archetypal ground. The address written by Jane Crofut's minister begins, so to speak, at the level of Jane Crofut's life, and where she lives is the same everyday world in which we live, too. But then the address moves beyond that and into, in order, the domains of geography, astronomy, and finally theology. The term *archetype* invokes "the Mind of God" because it designates an aspect of underlying, eternal order. Such order is beyond ordinary folk-indeed, it is beyond all human beings. It may be described as "the Mind of God," or it may be represented by Plato's conception of ideal forms. Such things are not knowable, and something that is not knowable may as well not exist. But the archetypes do manifest themselves in our lives, in our daily round. Rather than continuing this abstract discussion, I turn instead to a concrete instance of the manifestation of a particular archetype in a tiny poem. It is a haiku by Ezra Pound:

> In a Station of the Metro
>
> The apparition of these faces in the crowd:
> Petals on a wet, black bough. (2003, 287)

The image presented is clear enough: we can see the train in the station punctuated by windows which reveal to us the faces of people illuminated by the lights inside the cars. Their faces are visible to us, but transitory; the train will leave the station and they will be gone: a common sight for anyone living in a city with an underground transit system. But obviously something else is going on here, something beyond the literal experience. The image of the petals reminds us of the transitoriness of spring, of generativity, of beauty. The blackness of the bough suggests not only the black railroad car but the larger, ominous overtone of death: the train will pull out, the people will be gone. The poem has prepared us for this reminder of mortality: it is the *apparition* of these faces—the petals—that we are seeing. The word "apparition" suggests ghost, spirit, something not of this world, something of questionable solidity, something perhaps menacing. As the Oxford English Dictionary says, "The supernatural appearance of invisible beings ..." (1989, 2nd ed.).

We do not think much about the fact that in the midst of life we are in death. But it is a fact, and it remains a fact whether we think of it or not. We are here dealing with the archetype of the journey, the journey we are all on. This is reinforced by the setting of the poem—the Metro station. To repeat: archetypes are principles, like the idea of journey, that are present all the time and for everyone. Archetypes are universals. They cannot be described concretely in themselves, because they are abstractions, generalizations, ideas; but they are represented in experience all the time. We cry at a wedding because we are in the presence of the archetype of wholeness, represented by a union of opposites, and we have a deep longing for such a union in our own life, and in our own mind. To the extent that we are in awe of that longing and moved by it, we weep. At such moments—in theater, art, or life—we experience an archetype.

Pound's haiku started us on our way. In it, we find a vision, if you will, that is universally applicable. Petals on a black bough: ephemeral life arranged on a structure that will outlast the petals, and the fruit, and the season. The idea that life is transitory is obviously universal, as is the association of the spring season with life's beginning, and the association of the wet, black bough by itself with winter—not a part of the poem, but a part of our temperateclimate experience. At the same time, the poem brings to us an idea, and a feeling, that typically reside below the level of conscious awareness. So it is with archetypes; they are paradoxically familiar and unfamiliar. Familiar, because they are universals: mother, father, the seasons, light and dark, up and down. But unfamiliar, because we do not often *consciously* ponder the larger meanings in these things. Our conscious mind seeks the familiar. Universals are numinous; the familiar is humdrum, routine, ordinary. It is its unexpectedness that gives Jane Crofut's address such force. That, and its universality. The archetypes are this way, too. They are unexpected when we encounter them, and they seem to "arise" from some deeper understanding, some enhanced vision. Note *deeper*. Ego-consciousness likes to think that it is sufficient in itself, that it contains everything that we need for our lives. Thus we live on the surface. But one day we go to a museum and our thoughts are arrested, say, by the sight of a thirteenth-century painting of the Madonna and the infant Christ. We see in the mother's face both joy and sadness, and we know she knows what is to come; and in the infant's face we see an unexpected age, a mature loving, while at the same time the infant reaches towards his mother's face in the way babies do. The painting takes us *out of time*. It is not a snapshot of a mother and child. It has its own magically contradictory content of time present and time future, all in one image. It is more than our convention-conditioned ego can take in; we are suddenly disoriented, lowered, for the moment, into the archetypal depths of love and death, fear and hope, loss and redemption.

The archetypes are both universal and timeless. Hence they are often represented by gods and goddesses. In the Greek pantheon, for example, Zeus is father, Hera is always wife and Aphrodite is love, Apollo intellect, and so on. Except for Hermes—the trickster, among other things—each god or goddess stands for one, and only one universal. In real life, mother is a person, and idiosyncratic; but the mother archetype is all mothers, all origins, mother earth, the source. Each archetype can therefore be thought of as an idea, but the word "idea" does not suggest the emotional content: "mother" is not only origin, but comfort and security, too, at least in principle.

Biology speaks of instincts, patterns of response to the environment that are innate, built into the nervous system. The archetypes are similarly built in and universal, but the effect that an archetype will have on any one of us is determined both by the archetype itself and by our own particular experiences with it. We all have a sense of mother and origin, but we also have our own memories of these things. Much of this book is about how particular experience colors our sense of the archetypes. Andrew Samuels and Fred Plaut write:

Archetypal patterns wait to be realized in the personality, are capable of infinite variation, are dependent upon individual expression and exercise a fascination reinforced by traditional or cultural expectation; and, so, carry a strong, potentially over-powering charge of energy which is difficult to resist (someone's ability to do so being dependent upon his stage of development and state of consciousness). Archetypes arouse affect, blind one to realities and take possession of will. (1986, 26–27)

Consider the idea that archetypes "wait to be realized in the personality." This says that there are structures outside of a particular psyche that are constant in human nature, in the same way that the ability to walk upright is such a constant. The archetype is not just an idea; it is also a container for developmental potential. This is one place where the resemblance of archetype and instinct becomes clear. For example, a newborn lying on its back will, when startled, reach out with both arms and then seemingly clutch itself, as if trying to hold on to something: the "Moro reflex" (Crain, 1985, 38). The need to *hold on* is a universal one, as is the need to be held. But what, precisely, is inherited? Not, certainly, images per se. Not, probably, innate or "hard-wired" structures, such as Noam Chomsky's proposal of an innate syntactic theory. Current thinking, exemplified by George Hogensen (2001) and Jean Knox (2003), proposes a developmental model, dependent upon reliably experienced events which result in the accretion of consistent and universal early psychic structures. These structures are then elaborated and modified by the actual experience we call "growing up." Exactly how this process works is of enormous theoretical importance, but it is not a focus of my discussion. I am concerned more with how we experience archetypes, and less with why that experience occurs. Therefore, in order to avoid cumbersome and repetitive caveats, I will write throughout as if archetypes and the archetypal ground exist. The question whether they exist a priori or are formed by interactions of experience and psyche, I leave to researchers such as those I have just cited.

The archetype is a principle. There is a universal principle of father and fathering, but there is no "generalized father." There are only particular images, descriptions and examples of fathers. The archetype is invoked when, for instance, we refer to a priest as "father," or when we describe Niagara as "the Father of Waters." The realm of the archetypes is "the Mind of God" on Jane Crofut's envelope. Trying to contemplate that will make clear the futility of trying to envision or comprehend the archetype in itself. We must be content with manifestations of archetypes, in myth and art and dream and fantasy, and in the body, in affects—like crying at the wedding. In our daily life, archetypes manifest themselves in the same three ways that the unconscious does: in dreams, in the body, and in those moments when we are in the grip of a complex. (More about complex in the chapter concerned with early adulthood.) All of these are concrete experiences that connect back to their archetypal final cause.

Archetypal images—the mother and child, for example—are created in all cultures and in all periods of history: Mary and Jesus, Isis and Horus, Demeter and Persephone, the divine child and the wise old woman. Jung argued that the universality of the archetypal ground explains the fact that such images are ubiquitous in dreams, and in the fantasies of psychotic patients.

Again, "Archetypal patterns wait to be realized in the personality...." Those patterns are eternal, unchanging, like the Platonic forms, or "the Mind of God." A metaphor may illustrate the relationship between the archetypes and an individual. Suppose all the archetypes are arranged on a template. Now imagine a human being. That human being is born with, and will immediately amplify (literally, in synapses), his or her particular pattern of receptivity which, over the course of a lifetime, interacts with the template. The interactions begin at birth, or perhaps even in utero. The history of the person's life may be written as a series of encounters between the archetype and each particular experience of it. We live our lives in contact with the template of archetypes, and the specific ones that we "pick up" will be determined by where we happen to move on that template, and for how long.

For obvious reasons, some archetypes, like father and mother, are picked up by everyone, but the form they take in the psyche, and the force the archetype has, will depend on the individual's life with father and mother. What about orphans? Wordsworth, who lost his parents, found parental archetypes in lake, tree, and cloud. Such is the force that links archetype, as spirit, with instinct, the body. To repeat: The relationship between the archetype and any given person's recognition of it is entirely dependent upon the particular circumstances of that person's life. The archetype and "real-time" experience meet up, and the consequence of that meeting lives on uniquely in that individual psyche. I provide instances throughout: my amplification of my own first marriage shows a mother complex (on both sides) shaping its history and outcome, and my second marriage is (among other things) a bringing together of two people who, because of early times of abandonment and not being seen, were living out lives in search of some assurance of the reality of their own being—the archetype of the questing wanderer. My first marriage was much more "unconscious" than the second. The more we can *know*—that is, be conscious of—the less power the archetype will have over us.

But consciousness is always limited. People who try to live as if consciousness is everything become helpless or fearful when the unconscious asserts itself. Psychiatrists are often viewed skeptically by other physicians: the world of mental illness is mysterious when compared with the more rational and concrete worlds of internal medicine or surgery. My work in hospitals showed me that for internists or surgeons the world of the Intensive Care Unit, with its beeping monitors and flashing lights and intubated patients with their wheezing breathing machines and the constant threat of death, was a more comfortable place than the inside of a locked psychiatric ward, where the sights and sounds may consist simply of a few patients in the day room watching *The Oprah Winfrey Show.* Another example from art: life lived in proximity to the unconscious has its resonances within the atonal music of Schönberg and the paintings of Kandinsky; they knew one another, revered each other's work, and suffered from the scorn of the ordinary public. Living thus, let alone creating, on the border between conscious and unconscious makes for a certain estrangement, a feeling of disconnection from society, the collective. One of life's tasks is to maintain a creative tension between conscious and unconscious in spite of the sometimes painful loneliness that comes from being separated from ordinary worldliness by an awareness of one's inner world. Robert Frost:

> They cannot scare me with their empty spaces
> Between stars—on stars where no human race is.
> I have it in me so much nearer home
> To scare myself with my own desert places. (1976, 413)

King Lear once again provides us an illustration. At the start of the play, he has at hand a map of his kingdom. On it, he has divided that kingdom into three parts, and he announces his intention to step down and apportion it among his three daughters. If he were free of the archetype of kingship, he would proceed with the division in a rational way, and there would be no play. But he is not free: he still feels the "overpowering charge of energy" inherent in kingship. He cannot see that he has "desert places" within himself, because he has not yet experienced them. He is living out a one-dimensional kingship: all-powerful, always right. This sort of kingship contains power and power only. The concept of king has been linked with the sun, as noted in the following chapter's discussion of ancient Egypt. Louis XIV was the Sun King; the king connects with god, has divine right. To be crowned is to be at the height of achievement: Babe Ruth was "the Sultan of swat," and Elvis Presley was "the King." More generally, as John Weir Perry points out, the principle of kingship arose as civilization shifted from the agricultural community, with its diffuse social organization and its dependence on an "emotional investment in the fructification of the earth" [a matriarchal principle], to the city, the industrial community devoted to the accumulation of wealth and property. This new organization required a cohesive body politic, and that cohesion was assured by the presence of the king (1966, 17). Of all such instances the numinosity of the archetype of the king is assembled, over time, in history and psyche.

King Lear says he wants to let go of all this, but careful reading shows that this is not so. He starts his meeting with the lords and his daughters by announcing "Meantime we shall express our darker purpose." Then,

> 'Tis our fast intent
> To shake all cares and business from our age,
> Conferring them on younger strengths, while we
> Unburdened crawl toward death. Our son of Cornwall,
> And you, our no less loving son of Albany,
> We have this hour a constant will to publish
> Our daughters' several dowers, that future strife
> May be prevented now. (1986, I, 1, lines 38–44)

"Our darker purpose" is ominous; the fact that he inadvertently comes out with this in public shows his awareness of a vague menace, but also his unawareness of the actual situation within his unconscious, where a psychic king rules his mind. He next says that he, having been "unburdened," will "crawl toward death." This is suspiciously melodramatic, a narcissistic plea for sympathy. And then his real motives manifest themselves.

First, he demands that his daughters tell him, oldest first, how much they love him: "Tell me, my daughters... which of you shall we say doth love us most...." To rephrase this, undoing the royal *we:* "Which one of you will I choose as the one who most passionately speaks to me of my significance?" Far from giving up power, King Lear keeps all the power for himself. It is *his* choice that will determine the future of his kingdom and of his daughters. Whatever he may proclaim about giving up power, he is in fact giving up nothing, because he is gripped by the archetype of kingship. Something like this has happened to all of us, usually without so much at stake. We become arbitrary, stubborn, and angry. Then we wonder, afterwards "What came over me?" Whatever it was, it was partly outside of ourself, a force beyond our control, and we know that there is a whole gamut of such happenings, from falling in love to road rage. Thus the archetypes are never very far from ordinary experience, as "In a Station of the Metro" demonstrates. We live surrounded by suggestions of their existence. In the last year of his life, Carl Jung was interviewed for a film produced by the BBC. The interviewer asked Jung, "Do you believe in God?" and Jung replied, without thought or hesitation: "I do not believe. I know." This I take to be Jung's sense of the archetype. They are there. They wait to make themselves known.

The subject of this book goes beyond the assigning of archetypes to the particulars of one's life. Rather, it explores the idea that life embodies eternal patterns that we can come to know. We can then recognize them—in ourselves, in our relationships, and in the world at large. They give us a precious sense of the order of things. In each chapter I use autobiographical material by way of introduction or amplification, because I have both lived and observed (sometimes!) my own journey. This book, if written by a woman using female examples, would be completely different in many respects, but I am persuaded that its underlying argument for the universality of the archetypal ground would remain intact.

Whoever we may be, the present world-as-it-is, with everything in it from real war to media-driven distractions, pulls us away from reflection. The realm of the archetypes compels thought, quietude, awe, fear, and delight. They are indeed

> Those shadowy recollections,
> Which, be they what they may,
> Are yet the fountain-light of all our day,...
> (1948, 232)

CHAPTER 2

THE TIMELESS INFANT AND EARLY CHILDHOOD
THE FRESHNESS OF A DREAM

IT IS EXTRAORDINARILY difficult for most of us even to imagine, let alone recollect, particulars of what our earliest childhood felt like, and how the world looked to us, and how we experienced our parents, and our room, and the world outside the door. In "Intimations of Immortality from Recollections of Early Childhood," Wordsworth himself does not try to present us with specific details; he seeks to capture in more general terms the quality and meaning of his childhood world. The first four stanzas of Wordsworth's poem reflect what happens to any of us when we find ourselves in the presence of something—a landscape, a sound, a room—that carries us back in time:

> —But there's a Tree, of many, one
> A single Field which I have looked upon,
> Both of them speak of something which is gone...
> (1948, 232)

—and then, having been carried back, we feel again something of what it was like when we were very small indeed. We, too, are occasionally moved by faint echoes of our earliest experiences when they occur within our daily round. We go to a museum, say, with our spouse of many years, and we look up to find that the person we came with has disappeared—perhaps only momentarily, but nevertheless we feel an instant of loneliness, then abandonment: a minor-key bit of panic. This is early stuff, the infant alone in an empty room. Or, sitting in a quiet place—a church, perhaps—by ourselves, we unexpectedly feel comfortable, taken care of, in a larger, warmer way than we had expected. The origin of this is equivalently early. Such moments are not memories or recollections: they are embodied reconstructions of feelings infants have. "Embodied" is an important word. These feelings are in the physical body. We are not using our mind to remember or to ponder; instead, we have found ourselves in a place where these sensations come upon us all unbidden, unsought for. They happen in the same way that a breeze touching our cheek happens. It is a combination of bodily sensation and associated emotion. This is the world of the infant: a world defined entirely by sensation, by the body's continual recording of its immediate surroundings. The body is all; there is no reflection, no use of language, no awareness of awareness. There is no idea of "I," let alone "you." A baby's body and the world that surrounds it are, for the baby, the same thing, which is to say, everything. And everything is always and only now: there is no idea of past or future. To write about this early state is to create an illusion of understanding or remembering it, but neither specific memories nor understanding are in play. Here is Wordsworth's evocation of this state:

> There was a time when meadow, grove, and stream,
> The earth, and every common sight,
> To me did seem
> Apparelled in celestial light,
> The glory and the freshness of a dream. (1948, 232)

This is not so much descriptive as it is an exercise of nostalgia. It is a return to a way of being, rather than to a particular place. And that way of being is, I feel, the way an infant knows the world, and the way we, at night, know the world of our dreams.

Almost every dream we have is fresh; we have never had it before. Each night brings a new adventure. And even though this is true, the "I" within the dream—that is, the dream ego—almost always accepts the dream without questioning it or thinking about it, no matter how strange or frightening or blissful it may be. The dream ego, in short, apprehends the dream the way an infant apprehends everything: the world of the dream is just there as it is, as long as the dream goes on. The dream ego, like the infant, does not reflect. Here, as an example, is an actual dream:

> I am doing something with some older guys. One of them seems quite directive in giving advice about something I am to do. Then I and one of the guys are to go to catch a streetcar, like the old Magazine Street [New Orleans] car. But this one is more like a boat and runs alongside on a stream or canal with vegetation along it. We go to the end of the line to get it. There I see what is a cross between a barge, a skiff, and a long open streetcar. The sides are just a foot or so above the water. I step in and walk to the back and sit on the green wooden stern. Then a man who seems to be the driver comes on board.

There is much to be said about this dream, and we shall return to it in other contexts. For now, though, notice the dream ego's complete lack of reaction to that most curious boat/streetcar. For the dream ego, it is simply another fact, no more special than the older guys, or the driver. The parallel between the dream ego and the infant is obvious. For both, all experience is new experience, and so everything has equal force and effect. The infant and the dream ego possess a radical openness to everything. Openness is what Wordsworth celebrates at the beginning of his poem: "every common sight / To me did seem / Apparelled in celestial light,..." For the infant and the dream ego, it is always thus. What is the value of this openness? Why does it diminish as we grow older? Wordsworth has an answer for these questions, but the first four stanzas of his poem do not provide it. Quite the opposite: They leave us with nothing but a sense of loss, the loss of "a glory from the earth." Indeed, all he can do is ask,

> Whither is fled the visionary gleam?
> Where is it now, the glory and the dream? (1948, 232)

And, having thrust these great questions at his own psyche, he stopped writing. "This [The "Intimations" Ode] was composed during my residence at Town End, Grasmere; two years at least passed between the writing of the first four stanzas and the remaining part..." (1948, 1117). Wordsworth's questions may be rephrased as, "What has become of the completely open person I was as a child?" There is a devastating sadness to this inquiry. It is no wonder that Wordsworth needed two years before he could face it.

We will look, in due course, at Wordsworth's eventual answer. But he was, here, on the verge of another answer, as profound as his own will be. He just didn't see it. The fact is that a completely open person is always with us. He or she is to be found, in the character of the dream ego, in every dream we have. The dream ego. never judges or reflects or decides not to experience what's going on around it. In this way the dream ego is different from our waking ego. Our waking ego is almost always, so to speak, two people at once: one who does things, and another who reflects, or judges, or stands aside and watches. If the waking ego had experienced this streetcar/boat, it would have immediately asked something to the effect of, "What on earth is that?" In waking life, we adults are always aware that we are aware. Not so the dream ego. The dream ego takes everything as it comes.

Wordsworth was, as I have suggested, on to this, but not explicitly—that is, not consciously. Note again:

> There was a time when meadow, grove and stream
> The earth, and every common sight,
> To me did seem
> Appareled in celestial light,
> The glory and the freshness of a dream. (1948, 232)

Exactly so. A *dream*. And then he asks: "Where is it now, the glory and the dream?" Thus, running along underneath but parallel to the theme of loss, is the image of the dream, the dream world being the place where everything is purely taken in and never thought about or judged. Events, for the infant and the dream ego, simply yet deeply confirm existence itself, what D. W. Winnicott calls "going on being" (1965, 60), which means exactly what it says: the assurance, through the five senses, that one continues to exist. For an infant, subject to periods of terrifying aloneness, going on being is nothing less than life itself. And no matter what happens in a dream, the dream ego also goes on being.

At this point I turn to my own life for an example of going on being and its archetypal foundation. I combine my early history with the memory of a house my family has lived in since 1920. It is the place where I, as a child, encountered most vividly "every common sight. . . / appareled in celestial light." The house is in a summer community called Old Black Point, on the shore of Long Island Sound. I can go back there, in my mind, to images that do not change, that are for me timeless.

We live, all of us, with time and timelessness together. There is ordinary clock time, but underneath this there is timelessness. As I remember myself as a child I can see myself, swimming or running, and the image I see is endlessly repeatable: it defies clock time, as do snapshots or home movies. Whenever I return to my childhood place I go back in time, too. T. S. Eliot, in *The Family Reunion* (another return to a family home), has the chorus say:

> In an old house there is always listening,
> and more is heard than spoken.
> And what is spoken remains in the room,
> waiting for the future to hear it.
> And whatever happens began in the past, and presses
> hard on the future. (1939, 93)

This is a description of timelessness. Everything, past and future, is present. Clock time, though, is "real time," the time of consciousness, of the ego. It flows inexorably along, and the only "present" things are in the present moment. In contrast, the remembered, constant images we carry inside us are allied to the archetypes, those eternal abstractions in the collective unconscious. The unconscious is timeless, as you learn every time you dream of someone long dead who is nevertheless very much alive in the dream. And the archetypal foundation of the collective unconscious is timeless, too.

It is the archetypal that I experience in our summer home. My return to that home, summer after summer, isn't just a return to a place. It is also a return to the great archetypal patterns that underlie our lives whether we attend to them or not. I hope to show how my particular experience is also universal. I use my particulars because I know them; but you have yours, and yours have an archetypal foundation, too. If you feel something of your own as you read now, then for that moment you and I are on common ground, together within the objective psyche, the collective unconscious, shared by all humanity.

Of course I didn't know any of this, growing up. My parents and grandparents lived in the outer, extroverted world, as most people do in this country, not the inner one. As an introverted only child, I supplied my own narcissistic needs without knowing I was doing so. My conscious discovery of an inner world did not come until my sophomore year in college.

I came to Yale in 1951, intending to major in zoology. I was exempted from the freshman English course on the basis of a writing test, so I took a bunch of science courses in freshman year. In the following year I ran into the fact that a liberal education has to include stuff you don't want to study: there was a required literature survey course. I was immediately taken with the teacher, a man named William Madsen. The course, a mishmash of unconnected readings, was designed as "literature for scientists and engineers." In November we got on to T. S. Eliot's "The Love Song of J. Alfred Prufrock." Something about it absolutely gripped me. We had to write a paper about the poem, and as I wrote I discovered why I was so moved. J. Alfred Prufrock, that sad, uncomfortably middle-aged man, was telling me about what was going on inside his head! For example, Prufrock thinks to himself,

> I should have been a pair of ragged claws
> Scuttling across the floors of silent seas (1936, 14)

I was thrilled. Not only because I knew about those crabs scuttling across the floor of the sea since we had crabs among the rocks on the shore at Old Black Point; more astonishing to me was realizing that I had been having Prufrock-like conversations with myself for as long as I could remember, but I had no idea that anyone else had such an inner world. The paper I wrote for Madsen—I wish I still had it—was called "Awareness of Awareness." Since I was a sophomore, I am sure it was sophomoric. Nevertheless Madsen caught my excitement. I changed my major to English, took Madsen's course in seventeenth-century poetry the following year, and went on to a completely rewarding career as a teacher and professor of English, all started when my experience of an inner life had been validated for me by a teacher and a poem.

Now this raises the question of why experience of an inner life needs to be validated. Those of you who are introverts by nature but who are surrounded by extroverts will have a pretty good idea of why. My inner life began, as everything does, at birth. But my particular "birth-story" included an explicit denial, by the adults around me, of the very inner life that came to claim my attention in the most vivid ways, to some extent as a teacher of literature, but much more so later on, as a psychoanalyst. I tell the story of my own beginnings because of this very early chasm that opened up between my way of being in the world and that of my parents; I was the opposite of both of them, extroverted as they were. In the same way I was also the opposite of most of the other people I knew, whether they were my age or older. But here I begin with some family history.

My mother's parents rented a summer house on Old Black Point in 1916, and in the early '20s they bought a large house on the western shoreline of the point. My grandfather was a physician, specializing in tuberculosis, with his practice in New York City. He became a leader in the field; he was head of the TB ward at Bellevue and president of the New York Academy of Medicine; he discussed health policy with President Roosevelt; he had famous patients—an opera singer, the president of the Philippines, and Eugene O'Neill—and poor patients, for whom he provided a ferry boat in the summers, anchored in the East River for the fresh air. But in the summer— every summer—he vacationed at Old Black Point, occasionally writing articles but mainly playing tennis, croquet, and bridge, and taking part in the social whirl—lots of cocktail parties, and the sort of dinner parties no one does any more. He and I had a good, thoughtful connection. One June I had to be shipped off to a camp so I could be tutored in algebra. I felt awful the day I was to be driven there by my mother. My grandfather, who had a prodigious reputation as an intuitive diagnostician, said, "That boy is sick." "Nonsense," my mother replied. "He just doesn't want to go to math camp." So off we went. Even though there was some truth in what my mother said, nevertheless I gave almost the whole camp measles. (In my family almost everything that is remembered is embedded in a humorous story, the better to conceal any shadowy element.)

My grandparents both grew up in New Jersey, and they knew they would marry early on. To situate them in time, my grandmother knew an elderly man who, as a child, had met George Washington, and my grandmother's church had the first electric light ever installed in a public building—Thomas Edison's laboratory was just down the road. In 1969, watching Neil Armstrong walk on the moon, she remembered that bare bulb dangling at the end of a wire. She kept her own daily notes in a Guest Book, a sort of diary of the summers at Old Black Point. My favorite entry is for August 9, 1945: "President Truman announced war is over! Had a picnic supper on terrace."

My mother and her older sister were first brought to Old Black Point by their parents when my mother was twelve years old. Summer communities, with their "summer houses," were part of the custom of the day for well-to-do families. There were famous resorts like Newport or East Hampton or Fishers Island, and then there were newer and smaller ones, like Old Black Point. The slightly unknown aspect of the place has always appealed to me. By the time of my arrival in 1933, there were two Black Point communities. Ours was, of course, *Old* Black Point. The original idea had been to make a golf course on the other side of the point, but the plan fell through, and the land was bought up by a real estate developer, Jas. J. Smith. He created *New* Black Point, with its Black Point Beach Club. The distinction between the two was my introduction to class warfare, played out especially in viciously contested softball games when I was a teenager. We wore tennis shorts and sneakers. The New Black Pointers wore blue jeans and spiked baseball shoes. Out of such serious games a piece of the social aspect of the Jungian shadow formed in me, and no doubt in the New Black Pointers, too; we were shadow for each other.

My mother and father were married in 1931. My father had grown up in Englewood, New Jersey, graduated from Yale in 1926, and had a year at Trinity College, Cambridge, reading history. At Yale he had been captain of the baseball team, very important in those days, the sports-crazed Roaring Twenties. He was a superb hitter and had an offer to try out for the Boston Braves, but banking and stock brokerage looked a lot more promising. How times have changed! My mother grew up in New York City. She was the younger and more beautiful sister. At Bryn Mawr, she starred in track and field with Katherine Hepburn. *The New York Herald Tribune* published a photo showing the two of them, in bloomers, doing the high jump; they seem equally glamorous. But my mother soon dropped out to study painting with Walt Kuhn in New York. She painted all her life, and she had a grand retrospective exhibition at Old Black Point in 1994. But she also married my father, and had me, so her painting was compromised. Years ago, when I was in my twenties, my first wife's closest friend Helen was also studying art, when she fell in love with a dashing law student whose family were friends of my parents. Helen knew my mother had faced exactly this choice. She asked my mother, "Peggy, what should I do?" My mother said, "Helen, if you want to marry Charlie, marry Charlie. If you want to be an artist, be an artist." Helen has had dozens of suitors, has never married, and is a thriving artist in California. My mother made the other choice, a decision that hung in the air all the rest of her life. She was always aware of her unlived life, but she concealed the pain of that awareness behind a fabulously charming persona that mesmerized people. In our house at Old Black Point, in the summer of 1933, my mother was pregnant with me, my mother's sister was pregnant with my cousin, and a friend who was staying with them was also pregnant. I was due in late October, but my mother went into labor on August 28 and an ambulance was called. The ambulance driver came into the house and was confronted by one pregnant woman after another. He thought he'd come to a home for wayward girls. My grandfather was in New York, but a physician colleague accompanied my mother in the ambulance. The intent was to bring my mother to Bellevue, but, as my parents were fond of pointing out, I have a propensity to be early for everything: instead of making it to New York, I got off in New Haven. In the words of the chart notes from the Yale-New Haven Hospital:

> Lindley—baby boy. Admitted August 28, 1933.
>
> Admission note: White male newborn: Ref: Dr. Thoms. Cause: prematurity. History is inadequate. Mother supposedly at seventh month of gestation. Began to bleed and was starting down to New York when bleeding became more profuse, and she stopped in New Haven where examination indicated need for immediate delivery and c-section was done. Child cried spontaneously.

My mother, who had lost a great deal of blood, both before and during the surgery, was in very precarious condition after my birth, and was hospitalized for about two weeks. My grandfather came up from New York but did not arrive in time for the delivery. My grandfather's colleague watched the surgery from the little amphitheater that surrounded the operating room. After handing me over to the pediatrician, the obstetrician who'd delivered me and who had been so concerned with the bleeding said, to no one in particular, "Did anyone happen to notice the sex of that child?" My grandfather's associate replied: "I may not know my medicine, but I know my art. That child was a boy!" In my family this was always told as a funny story, but, at some level, I must have heard it as also saying how busy the obstetrician was with other things besides me (and no doubt he was). How common this feeling is: of wanting to be seen, of *needing* to be seen, while all the people nearby are so involved with each other as to seem oblivious to that need. For at the very moment that the obstetrician asked his question, I was not being seen, but I was seeing.

What is birth? I imagine it is, first, the shock of seeing—of light. Then of sound. It is light, though, that must be amazing to the infant at the moment of birth. (It is probably the more amazing for the cae-sarean-delivered infant. In a normal delivery, the baby's painful passage through the birth canal must have an initiatory quality to it. But in a Caesarean delivery, at least in the ones I've seen, the baby seems to pop out through the incision all at once.) In any event, consider for a moment that first burst of light. It is no wonder that birth supplies the conscious and unconscious background for all our creation myths. As Erich Neumann observes,

> Mythological accounts of the beginning must invariably begin with the outside world, for world and psyche are still one. There is as yet no reflecting, self-conscious ego that could refer anything to itself, that is, to reflect. Not only is the psyche open to the world, it is still [as we have seen] identical with and undifferentiated from the world; it knows itself as world and in the world and experiences its own becoming as a world-becoming, its own images as the starry heavens, and its own contents as world-creating gods.
>
> ... [I]n all peoples and in all religions, creation appears as the creation of light. Thus the coming of consciousness, manifest-

ing itself as light in contrast to the darkness of the unconscious, is the real "object" of creation mythology. (1970, 6)

None of this is known, let alone remembered, from birth; nevertheless it is embodied in the newborn. Again I emphasize the deep
meaning of "embodied." But if we do not have memories that can
be formed into language, we do have other people's accounts of our
birth and infancy. Out of these accounts we construct an image of
our own infancy. There is another image, what Daniel Stern calls the
clinical infant: the clinical infant is, for Stern, the patient-as-infant
that is imagined by both patient and therapist as they work together.
It is thus a construction made almost entirely of words, but with
occasional emotions and sensations in the body. As Stern says, "[The
clinical infant] is created to make sense of the whole early period of a
patient's life story, a story that emerges in the course of its telling to
someone else.... The story is discovered, as well as altered, by both
teller and listener in the course of the telling. Historical truth is established by what gets told, not by what actually happened" (1985, 15).
I would broaden this definition to include the ourself-as-infant that
we construct for ourselves. This infant is composed of stories we have
been told as well as images of places we lived, together with constellations of feeling—all of this left in our body like archaeological rel-
ics. It is our own infant imago, with the term imago here used in its
conventional psychoanalytic sense: the totality of the infant-we-were
that we still carry with us. "Family stories" are extremely important
building blocks for this. We listen to the witnesses. The closer the fit
between the anecdotes and the experiences, the more sure we are of
the quality and validity of our sense of the world. In other words, it is
a very bad thing, psychologically, to be lied to. This is not to say that
the experiences have to be "good" in order to have worth. The "quality of fit" between reality and anecdote is much more important than
whether the anecdotes we are told are peaceful and benign or chaotic
and troubling. If the "fit" is good we may be expected to develop a
retrospective trust in what we have been told, or are being told, by the

people, like our parents, who were there. An adult whose life is now being lived under a cloud of vague but troubling anxiety is not helped by being told (by her mother, say) that she was a "wonderful, happy" child if she was in fact an anxious one. In such cases, it is probably the mother who needs to construct this fiction in order to cover over her own anxieties and guilt about what actually went on in the early life of her child. Story is never mere anecdote: it is psychic history. Here, then, I take up mine; the chart notes continue:

A small but well-formed infant with infrequent weak cry and well marked cyanosis of nail beds and mucous membranes. Respirations are irregular and accompanied by marked inspiratory effort with extreme retraction of sternum. No attempt at complete exam made. Impression: prematurity. Atelectasis [defective expansion of the lungs] widespread. Treatment: McIlleny Tent, Oxygen.

10:15 P.M.: Color not good; oxygen tent. Breathing rapid but regular. 12:30 A.M.: Child was out of the O^2 tent about ten minutes, during the lysis [subcutaneous glucose and saline]. Given CO^2 and O^2 to which it would respond with better color, but at the end of the lysis, child stopped breathing and became very cyanotic, and showed no response. Given caffeine subcutaneously. No response. Given intracardiac adrenalin, [by injection], 1cc. Began to breathe about 15 sec. later and was put in O^2 tent. Breathing continued regularly and color returned. O'Donnell.

Dr. O'Donnell had just read an article about adrenalin (epinephrine) that afternoon in the hospital's library; no one knew much about it. Obviously he saved my life. My parents, who knew Dr. O'Donnell had been a famous football player for Yale, always said he had known what to do because he knew how to stick needles into footballs to blow them up.

By the following day I was improving. By the fifth of September I had an appetite: "Child takes his formula very well, still receiving

CO^2 and O^2, color maintained very well, cry is strong, general condition steadily improving." By the fifth of October it was noted that "He
takes formula very hungrily." In my family I've always had a reputation for loving food, as well as for arriving early. Such are the little
hilarities designed to paper over what the experience really was. There
is no record that any family member visited me during my stay in the
neonatal ward. I was discharged on October 23; I had been in the
hospital fifty-six days.

Does one remember these things? I believe all experience is
imprinted on the psyche; the word "remember" isn't quite it, though.
Remembering is too conscious, too much a function of the ego. Here
is Anne Sexton, from her poem "Dreams," contained in a group of
poems called *The Death Baby*:

> I was an ice baby.
> I turned to sky blue.
> My tears became two glass beads.
> My mouth stiffened into a dumb howl.
> They say it was a dream
> But I remember that hardening. (1974, 11)

"[T]hat hardening" is what I think I carry with me, my way, perhaps,
of dealing with abandonment, with being orphaned. Edinger (1972,
132) observes that orphans develop a "hole in the psyche" through
which they see the archetypal parents. I saw, through that hole, Old
Black Point as my whole archetypal realm: it was a containing, nur-
turing world. Its shoreline and waves and tides and rocks and stars
held me and reassured me with their ever-returning patterns. As
Wordsworth did, I found parents in nature.

Let me explain by first saying something about my actual mother
and father before and after my birth. I've indicated that both were
golden people; good looking, wealthy enough, successful. They
knew how to have fun and were very popular. Although my mother
had many beaux, my father was charming and persistent; I think my
mother also knew he had fallen for her so completely that she would

continue to have the sort of power over him that a woman who is carrying her partner's positive anima always has. We speak of *falling* in love, thereby acknowledging its profoundly unconscious nature. As we fall asleep, so we fall in love; the direction of the unconscious is downward, away from ego and therefore away from light, from reason. I think he felt lost, but innocently, blissfully lost. Golden people, in a golden time.

My birth, or rather my mother's Caesarean, changed all that. My mother nearly died. My father, frightened and appalled, decreed they would have no more children, although my mother could have had more children and said (years later) that she wanted to. My mother's survival was much more of an issue than mine. When I was finally taken home I was put in the care of a nanny. The orphan experience was thus continued. I saw my parents seldom, and always when they were engaged in something else: getting ready for a party, leaving in the car, talking incomprehensibly. The distance they put between themselves and me was part of the culture; it was common for children like myself to be cared for by nannies in those days. But at a deeper level, I was the death child. My mother's near-death (caused by me) was the first encounter either of my parents had had with real terror, pure shadow for them. They could not look at the infant me without also remembering that terror. Not that they were in any way abusive or neglectful. Not at all. Instead, they were removed, charming, distant—very distant. A portrait my mother painted of me when I was two shows this: I look down, and away. We do not see each other. And we didn't. So I reacted as an introverted only child often does. I concluded (unconsciously) that the only really intimate relationship I could have was with myself. Black Point was for me a perfect setting for the growth of this relationship. It was a place where I could *become*. The child is the reality, and the image, and the archetype, of becoming. In Old Black Point, things became. Alone as I was, I grew, but remained an infant, too. That is why I go to my own childhood in this chapter rather than in the chapter on childhood which follows. Still today, I walk into the summer house

and, if the door to the terrace is open, I can feel the salt breeze from the Sound, and I can hear small waves breaking and dissolving into foam among the tangles of seaweed and rocks that line the shore just below the house.

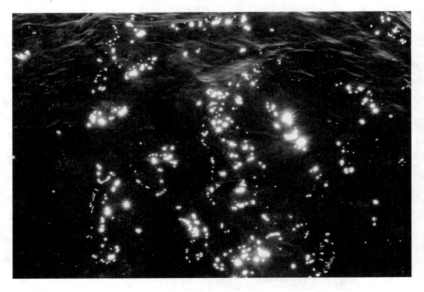

I see objects: a painting, a lamp, a table, an antique clock, candlesticks. They evoke people. My grandmother remembering a trip to buy the clock. Or they evoke my own associations. The bubbles in a glass ornament become, in my imagination, a firmament of stars.

A child such as I was, returning each summer to the same place, becomes lost in sameness. I made my own time, as an only child will, because, as I've said, my parents had their own life, more fun and more rewarding for them than a small boy could be. So I created a world for myself and lived in it, quite happily; what I was missing went into the dark. Time stopped its flowing, and the moment of the house stretched out. The past—of school, of schedules—was gone, and the future became unnecessary or irrelevant all summer long.

When we work with a dream, we often notice that there is no linear or logical time within it: people long dead appear and talk, or historical figures visit with us. From this we know, as I have said, that the unconscious is a timeless realm. The Black Point house was, for me, timeless and unchanging, as were the summers, and so the house became an analogue of the unconscious, the place where dreams originate.

There was one momentous exception, which I found exciting, more than frightening. In 1938, a hurricane shook the walls, and wind and rain stripped leaves from the trees and plastered the south side of the house with them; a gigantic willow tree fell; gales peeled shingles off the roof and water streamed into the attic and then through bedroom and living-room ceilings; waves and the high tide bent the terrace doors and sea water washed through the hall; we could not hear ourselves over the voices in the wind.

The storm passed; repairs were made. The house, like psyche itself, was both vulnerable and inviolable, moving and still unmoved.

I the child, in the seemingly endless summer, dropped into the infant's timeless archetypal ground. But that same child, growing and exploring in this unvarying place, found himself caught up in the inexorable flow of time represented by learning to swim, learning to ride a two-wheeler, learning to drive, to kiss. One summer an aunt died in her sleep. A few summers later my grandfather, surrounded by medicines and IVs, died in another upstairs room. Years later, when my father, a lover of landscapes and gardens, lay dying in that same room, he could see, outside his window, a maple tree I'd just that summer planted for him to replace a deteriorated apple tree. It flourishes now, shading the terrace. Each year I grow older, but each year the tide pools among the rocks fill and empty; each year the sun sets into the sound, beyond Griswold Island or Hatchett's Point, and each year, in the gathering darkness, the herring gulls and the cormorants begin their squawking nightly choruses from distant rocks and from rookeries on nearby islands, first in unison and then quieting mysteriously, only to start again; each year, lying in the dark with the bedroom window open for the sea air, I listen, and wonder.

The rocks on our shore drew me.

I studied them, learned about minerals, and began to collect quartz and feldspars and micas, components of the granite that Black Point is formed from. When I was still quite small (maybe ten years old) my father's mother, who had a magical ability to see an adult inside the child I was, gave me a copy of Dana's *Manual of Mineralogy* for Christmas, and I was entranced; I learned crystallography and chemical formulas. I went often to the Museum of Natural History in New York during the winters and studied their wonderful mineral collection, in those days displayed in endless glass cases with handwritten labels for thousands of specimens. Think of it: I went by myself, walking across Central Park from our apartment on East 76th Street. Nowadays a child wouldn't be allowed to do that, and nowadays anyway the museum has turned its mineral hall into a glitzy, dark media showcase, full of taped narratives and videos, the showy specimens all theatrically lit, giving a little boy no chance to just explore, and find things on his own.

Three other fascinations developed for me at about the same time. One was the microscope. I had a toy microscope and collected all sorts of algae and seaweed from our shore; again, I had books, and tried to learn the names of what I was looking at. I also spent hours in the attic of Dr. Lambert, the doctor who had noticed I was a boy. His house was just down the shore from ours. He had not only a wonderful old microscope but a huge collection of histology slides he'd saved from medical school. I looked at sections of liver and kidney and esophagus and adrenal gland, and at one slide whose label ominously read, "heart muscle from man executed at Sing Sing."

Another fascination was with astronomy. I would set up a small telescope on our front lawn every clear summer night. I learned constellations and how to find easy double stars, like Albireo, and objects like the Andromeda nebula or the star cluster in Hercules. In the winter my mother took me to the Hayden Planetarium. She maintained she enjoyed it; I loved it. I identified so completely with the lecturer that I've wondered since if that wasn't part of my deciding to become a teacher. These days, of course, that experience is gone, too: planetarium shows are computerized and feature the disembodied voice of Leonard Nimoy or William Shatner, or Tom Hanks.

The third fascination was with ancient Egypt, particularly with the Egyptians' belief in an afterlife. I haunted the basement of the Metropolitan Museum of Art, where the mummies were. As my life had begun with the near death of myself and my mother the

Egyptian afterlife seemed a comfortable place indeed, and very real, unlike heaven as presented in Sunday School. The "big rocks" at the Old Black Point beach reminded me of the tomb of Perneb, installed at the entrance to the Metropolitan's Egyptian galleries. It contains reliefs of offerings and the false door through which the soul returns to replenish itself from the stacks of bread and game pictured on the walls. A wonderfully ordinary eternity.

At Black Point, then, I oscillated between these polarities: rocks and minerals, the inanimate concrete objects of the earth, on the one hand; and stars and planets, so huge and so distant, on the other. And, behind these, life and death. I grew up with science, and then discovered poetry. Both domains produce symbols, and thus an inner life.

Again T. S. Eliot, describing a world both inner and other, a world to be forever explored:

> The river is within us, the sea is all about us;
> The sea is the land's edge also, the granite
> Into which it reaches, the beaches where it tosses
> Its hints of earlier and other creation: . . .
>
> (1944, "The Dry Salvages," 21)
>
> Home is where one starts from. As we grow older
> The world becomes stranger, the pattern more complicated
> Of dead and living. . . .
> Here and there does not matter
> We must be still and still moving
> Into another intensity
> For a further union, a deeper communion
> Through the dark cold and the empty desolation, . . .
>
> (1944, "East Coker," 17)

The archetypal references in the poems echo my particular experience of shore and rock, tide and sky. The echoes are constantly reassuring; they are dependable. They are *there*.

The process of individuation requires a space both safe and hazardous, known and unknown; a space charged with contradictions and opposites but nevertheless humane and sympathetic; a space in which the gestures and images of the inner life are honored and sustained, the whole informed by an idea of order. It is the space we deserve as children but seldom have. Such a space has immeasurable value. That is the space, I realize now, that I provided for myself at Black Point, and Black Point provided for me.

All this resonates with the concept of archetype, but life distracts. We are caught in what E. E. Cummings called "ropes of thing" (1954, 401). "Inexplicable" emotion is evidence, usually ignored, of an archetypal field. I didn't start training as an analyst until 1984, so most of my life was obviously spent in ignorance of the archetypal ground. But that ground was always there, in the house, on the shore, in the night sky. Thus in Black Point, as I've said, I felt the tension of opposites all the time: rock and star, private self and public parents.

This is the deep meaning of home. Home is the primary setting for the flowering of feelings even when they are contradictory and puzzling or mysterious. Everywhere else is to some degree public; only home is private space, space in which feelings, whatever they may be, are free to grow. I do not mean that those feelings will be necessarily positive; only that they are there: associations to rooms, to a clock or a china bowl or the odors of cooking, fears of sounds from down the hall. In the public realm all of us are constrained to a certain degree by the expectations of the anonymous public itself. At home this constraint diminishes, or even vanishes.

Thus home, not the larger world, is the scene of emotional possibilities. The outside world demands of us that we live for the most part by concealing emotion, the more so as we grow older. In the outside world, we must live what W. H. Auden termed "the necessary impersonal life" (1962, 80). We conceal the flow of inner feeling. By contrast, the infant's world teems with objects and impressions that will later release our intuition of the timeless realm of the archetypes. In the Black Point house, objects became numinous for me. Of course I can only imagine my experience of these things

in infancy. All I know is that they were there: a painting of my grandmother as a little girl; a silver case for wooden matches made in the form of a clam shell; a hat rack hung with my father's bizarre collection of caps. These objects became infused with feelings, with memories of people. If rocks and stars had the numinosity of the archetypal, these rooms and their objects held the passing, human stage. They carry, for me, the trace of numinosity left over from that time, in my infancy, when I was going about the magical task of creating them. What Jung called the transcendent function is a continuing awareness of the symbolic dimension of ordinary experience. And it is at home that this awareness most naturally begins, grows, and, with any good fortune, flourishes. Or did flourish, so that the memories of such awareness are still alive. As we grow older these early experiences fade away, diluted by the press of obligations and the necessities of the present.

So the vision of the archetypal ground dies away. But it can be recovered by going back to the images of home and letting them do their work at the level of feeling, the work they did in childhood. We all have our own rocks and stars, our inherited or chosen objects. For this reason, like Eliot,

> We shall not cease from exploration
> And the end of all our exploring
> Will be to arrive where we started
> And know the place for the first time.
> (1944, "Little Gidding," 39)

To "know the place for the first time" is to be confronted with something entirely novel to us. This is the infant's knowing. We seek the familiar out of inertia or laziness, and we try hard to force new experience into old, known categories. But once in a while, a new experience—a painting, a piece of music, an unexpected vista—gives us pause, because it is both as new now as our infant's world was and yet familiar. Such moments are in the double space of the present moment and the archetypal ground brought together. At any age, we can become, momentarily, the timeless child. Openness is everything. The dream, as Wordsworth intuited, is the gift of the new, "the visionary gleam."

That is what "know[ing] the place for the first time" is about. But what is "where we started"? Infants have been written about and studied for years, and much is known. What cannot be known, though, is the true nature of an infant's experience of the world. In place of knowledge, we have built an elaborate structure of assumptions about the infant's world, as we have seen. Here is one more instance of this. In psychoanalytic circles, it has been the practice to assume that the first relationship, that between the mother and the nursing newborn, is based on the biological fact of hunger and release from hunger: Freud's oral stage, or, more generally, what John Bowlby has called "the theory of secondary drive" (1969, 210). Bowlby quotes Freud: "The reason why the infant in arms wants to perceive the presence of its mother is only because it already knows by experience that she satisfies all its needs without delay." Well and good; but Bowlby goes on to cite the work of Konrad Lorenz on imprinting, in which he showed that goslings (and other animals) "imprinted" on people, moving cardboard boxes, and other objects, and followed them around, even though nourishment was never associated with them. Clearly there is an instinct for connection that has nothing to do with food or warmth or security. Bowlby goes on to cite Harlow's famous work with rhesus monkeys, in which these creatures developed a strong preference for a cloth non-lactating mother substitute over a wire mother substitute that provided milk. Bowlby's conclusion, that social interaction is really at the heart of infant development, is heartily accepted and richly amplified by the work of Stern, cited earlier. This is what Winnicott meant by his famous observation that "there is no such thing as a baby" (1975, 99). There is only the dyad of mother-and-baby, at the beginning.

At this point I invoke my own infant-image once more. When I imagine myself an infant I see myself as alone. Always alone. I lie in my crib, on my back, and I look up at the beams in the ceiling and feel the edge of a blanket. Or I am on my side, looking out of a window and seeing a streetlight. There is never anyone else there. Sometimes I can hear voices: adults in conversation, laughter floating up the stairs from the living room. None of this is associated with any feeling of loneliness or abandonment. I am alone, but I do not feel threatened by that fact. It is just how things are.

How could I be alone without a feeling of abandonment, without the threat of annihilation (Winnicott, 1975, 303) hanging over me? I believe that the "relationship" theory of early infant development is essentially an extroverted theory: it has to do with the necessary presence of *other people.* Having been taken care of by nurses in the hospital and then by a nanny at home, I probably had only a very tenuous idea of what other people really were; so, as I have said, I started down my life's path by being my own caregiver. An extrovert would find this deplorable, or sad, and would probably be angry.

I felt none of those things. This was just how the world was, and it was up to me to make what I could out of it. This calls into question, in an idiosyncratic and personal way, the position taken by Winnicott and Stern, that infant well-being depends on interpersonal, social interaction, first, of course, with mother. My situation led in a different direction: away from a mother, or indeed any person, and toward the timeless realm of the archetypes. Surrounded as I was by tides and rocks and stars, and the sound of waves along the shore, I found my place.

In Stern's description of the stages through which an infant progresses (1985, 11) he distinguishes between the *emergent* self (birth to two months), the *core* self (between two and six months), the *subjective* self (between seven and fifteen months), and, finally, the *verbal* self. Each stage has crucially important features. Within the concept of the core self, for example, is the developing sense, in the infant, of its own agency. The infant learns that *if* it acts in a certain way, *then* the outside world will "respond" in some dependable, consistent way. This is Pavlov in the nursery. If the outside world responds erratically, or if it does not respond at all, the consequences, for anyone, are devastating. The seeds of borderline personality disorder, that most intractable and painful of maladies, are sown by such inconsistencies. But if things are, in Winnicott's famous phrase, "good enough," then all is well. Such was the case for me, I imagine, both in the hospital and after my discharge. My sense is that the trauma of my birth distanced me from my parents, but that was something going on in their psyches, not mine. I was affected by it, of course, but not directly.

Thirty years later I made a snapshot of my father holding his first grandchild, my newborn son. He holds the tiny baby far away from him and looks at it with an astonished skepticism, as if he were holding a small firecracker with a lit fuse and trying to decide what to do with it. That, I think, is how my parents felt, but, as I have said, I was with them seldom, and I was taken care of well enough. I got through Stern's early phases, then, more or less well.

In spite of the research Stern cites, much of our knowledge of early infancy remains speculative. The Jungian theory of "original wholeness" in an infant, as described, for example, by Neumann under the symbolic umbrella of the uroboros (1970, 5–38) has an attractive, even seductive logic about it, but it represents more our projection onto the infant than a psychological universal. Such projections may very well be the foundation of the mother-infant relationship, but we have no way of knowing. It is only with the advent of language that the inner world of the child begins to become accessible. There is, however, one thing of which we may be sure. Infant and mother, and the infant alone, inhabit a world whose foundation is not accidental but archetypal. The baby, even the baby alone, is surrounded by eternal structures. Waves and tides, rocks and stars; not literally, but symbolically, awaiting language. Without a shred of evidence, I can imagine that I, even as a newborn, had dreams. Those dreams were waiting for me to dream them. I was given time and space in which to do so. That, alone, is no small thing.

The larger point is that openness to all experience is the defining attribute of our earliest life in the world. "Everything," by definition, includes the archetypal ground. Wordsworth sums this up with economy and force:

> Our birth is but a sleep and a forgetting:
> The soul that rises with us, our life's star,
> Hath had elsewhere its setting,
> And cometh from afar:
> Not in entire forgetfulness,
> And not in utter nakedness,
> But trailing clouds of glory do we come
> from God, who is our home:
> Heaven lies about us in our infancy!
> (1948, 232, lines 58–66)

"Clouds of glory" may be thought of as the archetypes. Here Wordsworth, after those two years of questioning, finds his answer to the problem of whither has fled the glory and the dream. They have not fled; rather, they are lost sight of as a consequence of growing up; specifically, of growing away from the initial state of the infant's openness to everything.

"Heaven lies about us in our infancy!" The rest of our life, if things continue to go well enough, is a story of leaving this state behind and then returning to it. That return is both burdened and illuminated by consciousness. Consciousness is revealed in language, whether or not it depends upon it. And language, in turn, is what makes a society—a social setting—possible. That social setting raises the possibility that the world as created by an individual infant's proximity to its particular set of archetypes may not be the only world. This, when it comes, is a stunning discovery, and does indeed involve a profound loss, the loss of the proximity to heaven. But this is childhood, not infancy. In "Fern Hill," Dylan Thomas (1953) presents us a description that captures the essence of the heaven that lies about us in our beginning:

> And then to awake, and the farm, like a wanderer white
> With the dew, come back, the cock on his shoulder: it was
>   all
> Shining, it was Adam and maiden,
> The sky gathered again
> And the sun grew round that very day.
> So it must have been after the birth of the simple light
> In the first, spinning place, the spellbound horses walking
>   warm
> Out of the whinnying green stable
> On to the fields of praise. (1953, 179)

The infant, just by seeing and hearing and feeling, creates the world.

CHAPTER 3

THE CHILD
BEST PHILOSOPHER

H ERE IS WORDSWORTH'S tempered description of growing up:

> Shades of the prison-house begin to close
> Upon the growing boy,
> But he beholds the light, and whence it flows,
> He sees it in his joy;
> The youth, who daily farther from the east
> Must travel, still is Nature's priest,
> And by the vision splendid
> Is on his way attended;
> At length the man perceives it die away,
> And fade into the light of common day.
>
> (1948, 232)

As we have seen, Wordsworth intuited that the archetypal ground, those "clouds of glory," are the property of the infant. Just which clouds, and how they will affect us, will be determined by the particulars of our lives. Wordsworth would have found a kindred spirit in Jung, who wrote,

> [Man] is not born as a *tabula rasa*, he is merely born unconscious. But he brings with him systems that are organized and ready to function in a specifically human way, and these he owes to millions of years of human development.... Man brings with him at birth the ground-plan of his nature, and not only of his individual nature but his collective nature. These

inherited systems correspond to the human situations that have existed since primeval times: youth and old age, birth and death, sons and daughters, fathers and mothers.... Only the individual consciousness experiences these things for the first time, but not the bodily system or the unconscious. For them they are only the habitual functioning of instincts that were preformed long ago.... I have called this congenital and pre-existent instinctual model, or pattern of behavior, the *archetype*. This is the imago that is charged with the dynamism we cannot attribute to an individual human being. (1970, 315)

Jung goes on to assert that the search (largely unconscious) for origins, for a return to nature and the earth, leads not only to "the realm of the archetypes"; they, in turn, represent the "inherent possibilities of the 'spiritual' or 'symbolic'...." It is thus no wonder that Wordsworth sees both spirit and symbol in nature. Here nature and instinct blend insensibly together. For most of us, our personal parents originally had the numinosity of gods and goddesses, and only gradually, as we took on their ways by growing up, did they lose for us their archetypal power. But Wordsworth, as we have seen, is something like an orphan, his parents having died when he was so young. Wordsworth discovered the archetypes in nature. They are, for him, as they were later for Jung, "truths that wake/To perish never." Evidently, in those two years when he was searching for the numinosity he felt he had lost, he saw the connection between *earth* (or "nature," as we now say) and *parent:*

> Earth fills her lap with pleasures of her own;
> Yearnings she hath in her own natural kind,
> And, even with something of a mother's mind,
> And no unworthy aim,
> The homely nurse doth all she can
> To make her foster-child, her inmate man,
> Forget the glories he hath known,
> And that imperial palace whence he came. (1948, 233)

In another passage, however, Wordsworth somewhat withdraws his projection:

> While earth herself is adorning,
> This sweet May-morning,
> And the children are culling
> On every side
> In a thousand valleys far and wide
> Fresh flowers; while the sun shines warm,
> And the babe leaps up on his mother's arm:—
>
> (1948, 232, lines 44–49)

Here, the earth adorns herself as a mother might, but then our attention is drawn to real children. As suggested by the last line in this passage, the mother archetype becomes to some degree conscious. True, the awe that always surrounds any archetype is no longer to be found in nature and so there is a sharp sense of loss ("Where is it now, the glory and the dream?") but there is also a new inner state. What was once magically "out there" has become the conviction "that in our embers/Is something that doth live" (1948, 232). In other words, "out there" is no longer the whole story. Here is a new awareness: there is a person who exists and who experiences the world. The fundamental idea here is simply *I am*. In short, consciousness.

What does it mean to become conscious? When does the child cease just sensing and combine sensing with knowing that one is sensing? In other words, when does consciousness begin? And why? And what does consciousness do to our experience of the archetypal ground?

I do not present myself as an authority on these matters. For my purpose here I wish to raise one large theoretical issue: the relationship between consciousness and language. The issue, more precisely, is whether consciousness is dependent on—that is to say, formed through—language. It is an important question because upon its answer depends our determination of when consciousness begins. At the moment of its beginning, infancy, as defined here, ends. The magical creation of the world by the infant stops, or is mitigated, by a new duality: there is an "I," and there is the outside world. I posit that an awareness of one's self as a separate entity is the hallmark of the end of infancy and the beginning of childhood. But what does "awareness of one's self" mean?

I depend for this discussion on Stern (already cited), on Antonio Damasio, and on Julian Jaynes. Stern writes, "I am suggesting that the infant can experience the *process* of emerging organization as well as the result, and it is this experience of emerging organization that I call the *emergent sense of self.* It is the experience of a process as well as a product" (1985, 45). He gives many examples, from recent observational research, which attest to such emerging organization. For example, one-month-old infants scan human faces: "When scanning live faces newborns act differently than when scanning inanimate patterns. They move their arms and legs and open and close their hands and feet in smoother, more regulated, less jerky cycles of movement. They also emit more vocalizations..."(1985, 63). Such data, for Stern, are evidence of the emergent sense of self. This stage is followed by the sense of a core self, which involves, among other things, the development of a sense of agency (1985, 70ff.). The infant can cause things to happen. This, of course, leads to the concept of self and other; the infant can cause another person to do something. After this is the infant's discovery that other people also have feelings, some of which are analogous to their own; what Stern terms the subjective self (p. 124ff). Finally, there is the appearance, in the second year of life, of the verbal self. Stern here makes a telling point:

> ...[I]n fact language is a double-edged sword. It also makes some parts of our experience less shareable with ourselves and with others. It drives a wedge between two simultaneous forms of interpersonal experience: as it is lived and as it is verbally represented. Experience in the domains of emergent, core—and intersubjective relatedness, which continue

irrespective of language, can be embraced only very partially in the domain of verbal relatedness. And to the extent that events in the domain of verbal relatedness are held to be what has really happened, experiences in these other domains suffer an alienation.... Language, then, causes a split in the experience of the self. (1985, 162–163)

This is another way of imagining the loss of the visionary gleam suffered by Wordsworth. Language takes us away from immediate experience. With language we can construct other realities that are both plausible and imaginable: "Let's go to the zoo" triggers a plethora of images and imaginings in the child who has been there before. The future has become manipulable.

I will argue that Stern's verbal self is the requisite ground for what I want to call consciousness. His earlier selves, crucial as they are, strike me as affirmations of the archetypal ground. There is an archetypal element in the configuration of the human face which makes for an unconscious experience of recognition, and so on. The question is, really, the meaning of the term "self." No doubt the healthy infant, with "good enough" mothering, manages these changes in its internal states, and no doubt these changes constitute constructions of mind as well as ways of taking in experience. But a sense of self, I am convinced, depends on the ability to reflect.

Antonio Damasio presents a nuanced account of the development of what he calls *core consciousness,* and it, too, raises the issue of language in relation to knowing:

How do we ever begin to be conscious? Specifically, how do we ever have a sense of self in the act of knowing? We begin with a first trick. The trick consists of constructing an account of what happens within the organism when the organism reacts with an object, be it actually perceived or recalled, be it within body boundaries (e.g., pain) or outside of them (e.g., a landscape). This account is a simple narrative without words. It does have characters (the organism, the object). It unfolds in time. And it has a beginning, a middle, and an end. The beginning corresponds to the initial state of the organism. The middle is the arrival of the object. The end is made up of reactions that result in a modified state in the organism.

We become conscious, then, when our organisms internally construct and internally exhibit a specific kind of word-less knowledge—that our organism has been changed by an object—and when such knowledge occurs along with the salient internal exhibit of an object. . . . By what sleight of hand is such knowledge gathered, and why does this knowledge first arise in the form of a feeling?

The specific answer I deduced is presented in the following hypothesis: *core consciousness occurs when the brain's representation devices generate an imaged, nonverbal account of how an organism's own state is affected by the organism's processing of an object, and when this process enhances the image of the causative object, thus placing it saliently in a spatial and temporal context. . . .*

In short: As the brain forms images of an object—such as a face, a melody, a toothache, the memory of an event—and as the images of the object *affect* the state of the organism, yet another level of brain structure creates a swift nonverbal account of the events that are taking place in the varied brain regions activated as a consequence of the object-organism interaction. The mapping of the object-related consequences occurs in first-order neural maps representing proto-self and object; the account of the *causal relationship* between object and organism can only be captured in second-order neural maps. Looking back, with the license of metaphor, one might say that the swift, second-order nonverbal account narrates a story: *that of the organism caught in the act of representing its own changing state as it goes about representing something else.* (1999, 168-170)

What we have here is a description of an oxymoron: nonverbal reflection. Nevertheless we must take seriously the hypothesis that there is generated, in the brain, an "imaged, nonverbal account" of an event occurring simultaneously outside and within. If this is consciousness, then language has no place in it. Is Wordsworth describing experiences of nature which, when he had them, were not "languaged" at all? Here I repeat the argument of the previous chapter: the infant's early openness is not related in any way to language. It is simply a given.

In summary: both Stern and Damasio use the word "consciousness" to describe links that form, in the synapses of the infant's brain, between predictability (the ability to imagine an outcome ahead of time) and the outside world. From the point of view of research into infant development, this makes perfect sense. It is also congenial with the work of E. C. Tolman (1951), who concluded years ago that rats who learned how to successfully navigate a maze so as to avoid dead ends and get the food pellet had constructed a mental image, what he called a "cognitive map," of the maze. I do not think there is much difference between Tolman's rats and Stern's and Damasio's nonverbal infants. Tolman found his rats to be "marvelous, pure and delightful" (240). So are infants. They can indeed be those things without having the ability to reflect on what they are doing, or seeing, or feeling.

I am concerned instead, as I have indicated, with the link between consciousness and awareness. Awareness, in my sense of the term, depends on one's knowing that one is aware. I think, therefore I am. For an explanation of how this comes about, I turn to Julian Jaynes, whose *The Origin of Consciousness in the Breakdown of the Bicameral Mind* (1976) sets forth a theory of the origin of consciousness that depends explicitly upon language. Indeed, Damasio says, "When Julian Jaynes presents his engaging thesis about the evolution of consciousness, he is referring to consciousness post-language, not to core consciousness as I have described it" (1999, 188). Exactly so. One way of understanding the difference between Stern and Damasio, on the one hand, and Jaynes, on the other, is that Stern and Damasio both understand consciousness as arising from within the individual. This is a theory based on introversion. Jaynes, by contrast, has a theory that depends on contact between self and others. This is a theory based on extroversion. The concepts of introversion and extroversion are C. G. Jung's (as is, I note here, his idiosyncratic spelling of "extraversion"). Jung's monumental work on psychological types (1971) reminds us that theory building is never the objective, dispassionately analytical procedure it is often assumed to be; rather, it is a product of the typological preference of the theory-builder. This does not make one theory right and another wrong; it just makes them different from one another. So this is an appropriate place for me to say again what my own typological preference is: I am introverted—very much so. I will have more to say about this shortly.

I turn now to Jaynes. I do so through the medium of a poem by Donald Hall. Here it is:

The Sleeping Giant
[A Hill, so Named, in Hamden, Connecticut]

The whole day long, under the walking sun
That poised an eye on me from its high floor,
Holding my toy beside the clapboard house
I looked for him, the summer I was four.

I was afraid the waking arm would break
From the loose earth and rub against his eyes
A fist of trees, and the whole earth tremble
In the exultant labor of his rise;

Then he with giant steps in the small streets
Would stagger, cutting off the sky, to seize
The roofs from house and home because we had
Covered his shape with dirt and planted trees;

And then kneel down and rip with fingernails
A trench to pour the enemy Atlantic
Into our basin, and the water rush,
With the streets full and all the voices frantic.

That was the summer I expected him.
Later the high and watchful sun instead
Walked low behind the house, and school began,
And winter pulled a sheet over his head.

(1957, 92–93)

There are two states of mind described in this poem. The first, presented explicitly, is a state of mind in which the giant exists. In the second, by implication, the giant is dead. Between the first and the second, school begins. Before school—that is, before contact with other sensibilities, other modalities of belief and understanding—the four-year-old child has constructed a world entirely of his own making. He does not know that others, in different circumstances, have constructed worlds different from his. For the four-year-old, in that summer before school, his construction is entirely sufficient. It explains what needs to be explained: because the giant is sleeping, it is plausible that he will, at any moment, wake up. (The child already knows this from his own experience.) We adults, with our implicit acceptance of our own ("superior") consciousness, will say to the child that he is "imagining things." But this is not the child's world at all. *In the child's world, there is no difference between what is imagined and what is real.* This is what Jaynes terms the bicameral mind. I will provide a summary of Jaynes' argument. His book, however, is so elegantly reasoned and so entertainingly written that it became a best seller when it was published, and this in spite of, or perhaps because of, its formidable title; therefore, some readers might put my book down at this point and take up Jaynes'. For others, here is my summary.

First, consciousness. "Subjective conscious mind is an analogue of what is called the real world. It is built up with a vocabulary or lexical field whose terms are all metaphors or analogs of behavior in the physical world..." (1976, 55). Indeed, as Jaynes explains, we describe the mind itself metaphorically: we "see" a solution to a problem, or we "see the light" or we remain "in the dark." These are metaphors for consciousness at work. We "point out" an idea, or a word "is on the tip of my tongue," or, if I don't know something, I "draw a blank." In all these instances, I am *describing myself doing (or thinking) something.* In order to be able to do this, I have created what Jaynes terms an *analogue I.* The "I" that has "seen the light" is not at all the totality of who I am; it is a character I have invented so that I can use him to enact the mental feat I am trying to describe to someone else, or even only to myself. This "I" is, in other words, the part of me that I imagine doing things. We do this so often and so habitually that the analogue "I" blends insensibly into the totality of who we think we are. But it is not a totality at all (1976, 54ff). For Wordsworth to be able to ask "Whither is fled the visionary gleam?" he had to be at once a person asking the question and another person who does not know the answer. The question itself is meaningless unless there is real loss to go with it. The analogue "I" didn't know the answer. That was the part of Wordsworth that was being a poet. That is why the poet stopped writing. But another, almost unconscious, "I" kept right on going, living, doing, and, two years later, the "analogue poet" was able to take up the problem with "our birth is but a sleep and a forgetting." It is plausible to imagine Wordsworth, at this moment, looking back in time and imagining his analogue "I" moving from sad bafflement to new understanding, and taking pleasure in the journey. This is consciousness: to be able to do something and at the same time watch oneself doing it; to understand and watch the understanding happen. In short, the conscious person is *aware of awareness.* They know that they know.

This brings us to what I take to be Jaynes's crucial point which, paradoxically, is a theory of what it is like not to have consciousness at all. A person without consciousness is a person with no analogue "I." This means that all experience is nothing more or less than what happens, moment by moment, in that person's world. World and mind are the same.

The little boy Donald Hall, scared by the sleeping giant who might at any moment awake, is our example. "I looked for him, the summer I was four." And more than looked for him: "I was afraid the waking arm would break/ From the loose earth." He does not say, "I imagined that he would wake up." The whole scene is a plausible, potentially very real event. This is what the world is like before consciousness. *Everything* is real. Everything, including imagined events, and dreams. Jaynes proposes that, historically, adults, too, had no analogue "I." Insightfully, he writes of the men described in *The Iliad*:

> We cannot approach these heroes [in *The Iliad*] by inventing mind-spaces behind their fierce eyes as we do with each other. Iliadic man did not have subjectivity as do we; he had no awareness of his awareness of the world, no internal mind-space to introspect upon. In distinction to our own subjective conscious minds, we can call the mentality of the Myceneans a *bicameral mind*. Volition, planning, initiative is organized with no consciousness whatever and then "told" to the individual in his familiar language, sometimes with the visual aura of a familiar friend or authority figure or "god," or sometimes as a voice alone. The individual obeyed these hallucinated voices because he could not "see" to do by himself. (1976, 75)

It is the *bicameral* mind because a pillar of Jaynes's argument is that the two hemispheres of the brain (the bicameral brain) have very different roles to play in the generation and interpretation of experience and language. In right-handed people, the left hemisphere is responsible for generating speech and is the locus of rationality, of "understanding," whereas the right hemisphere is the source of metaphor and image-making (imagination). But the right hemisphere also contains structures that can generate speech but which go unused. Why, Jaynes asks, should this be so? His answer (which I truncate severely) is that the right hemisphere was the source of those voices upon which bicameral persons depended for the ordering of their world. The voices were transmitted across the anterior commissure and were then "understood" by the left hemisphere (1976, 102ff.).

But the right hemisphere remains the image-generating side. Hall's giant is a right-hemisphere creation in the bicameral four-year-old Hall once was. Another instance of bicamerality at work is provided by a Hittite text that presents interpretations of dreams. It is organized thus:

> [If someone] sees in a dream ...
> [If some]one sees in a dream an ox ...
> [If some]one sees in a dream a calf ... (Mouton, 2004)

Note this most carefully. The dream is not "had." It is we who say, "I had a dream." Not the Hittite text. There, the dream is *seen*, in the same way that we would see a tree or a sunset. The dream is no different from any other experience. Ancient Egyptian accounts of dreaming are exactly like this. Here is the Egyptian conception of the dream, as described by Szpakowska (2003):

> Modern dictionaries of ancient Egyptian concur that the most commonly used word for dreams is *rsw.t*. [This is a transliteration of hieroglyphic symbols. There are no vowels in hieroglyphic writing.] ...
>
> As a first step towards understanding the Egyptian concept of dreams we should first note that *rsw.t* is always a nominal form, a substantive "dream," and it does not have a corresponding verbal form in ancient Egyptian. In English, dreaming can be an activity; "I was dreaming," or "I dreamt last night," or it can be a substantive, as in "I had a good/bad dream." This is not the case in ancient Egypt, however,... (2003, 15)
>
> It appears that a dream in ancient Egypt is something seen, not done.... The ancient Egyptian saw ... the dream in the same way he would see the world, so there was therefore no need of a special verbal construction to denote an activity of "dreaming," or an exceptional verb for "seeing." This is confirmed by textual evidence which offers no examples of a verb "to dream."...

The ancient Egyptian dream is not an event rising from within the dreamer or an activity performed by an individual, but rather has an objective existence outside the sleeper's will. The use of the phrase "seeing in a dream" also indicates that the dream is an alternative state or dimension in which the waking barriers to perception are temporarily withdrawn. (2003, 20–21)

In other words, the dream ego in ancient Egypt is itself bicameral. Upon reflection this should come as no surprise. Just as, in the bicameral child, the image of the giant arising from the earth becomes a frightening reality, so the Egyptian sees the dream. Our consciousness causes us to think of dreams as having happened in us. Bicameral civilizations knew no "inner" experience at all. All experience came from the outside world. The Egyptian way of describing the dream is evidence of their bicamerality.

My thesis here is that the great experience of childhood is the transition, as so poignantly captured in Hall's poem, from the bicameral mind to the conscious mind. For Jaynes, that transition is brought about when one bicameral civilization (ancient Egypt, say) encounters another *but different* bicameral civilization (Crete, for instance). To their mutual horror and dismay, each discovers that the other has been hearing *different voices!* For the first time, the idea begins to form that perhaps the same voices are not heard throughout the whole world, or the whole universe, for that matter. Perhaps they come from inside! Perhaps *I* cause them! The summer of the giant ends when school begins: school, with other children, some of whom have never even thought about this giant, or indeed any giant. If Hall is Egypt, the other children (or even just one other child) represent Crete. Thus the bicameral mind metamorphoses into a dual mind contained in one person: the knower and the thing known, the believer and the thing believed; a person not blended into the universe but able to reflect about that universe. We move from the infant to the bicameral child and, finally, to the conscious child.

I turn first to the bicameral child and then to the bicameral mind, because I see bicamerality as a natural and necessary phase between the timeless infant and the conscious person. Here is Wordsworth's description of the bicameral child:

> Behold the child among his new-born blisses,
> A six years' darling of a pygmy size!
> See, where 'mid work of his own hand he lies,
> Fretted by sallies of his mother's kisses,
> With light upon him from his father's eyes!
> See, at his feet, some little plan or chart,
> Some fragment of his dream of human life,
> Shaped by himself with newly learned art;
> A wedding or a festival,
> A mourning or a funeral;
> And this hath now his heart,
> And unto this he frames his song:
> Then will he fit his tongue
> To dialogues of business, love, or strife;
> But it will not be long
> Ere this be thrown aside,
> And with new joy and pride
> The little actor cons another part;
> Filling from time to time his "humorous stage"
> With all the persons, down to palsied age,
> That life brings with her in her equipage;
> As if his whole vocation
> Were endless imitation.
>
> Thou, whose exterior semblance doth belie
> Thy soul's immensity;
> Thou best philosopher, who yet does keep
> Thy heritage, thou eye amongst the blind,
> That, deaf and silent, read'st the eternal deep,
> Haunted forever by the eternal mind,—
> Mighty prophet! Seer blest!
> On whom those truths do rest,

Which we are toiling all our lives to find,
In darkness lost, the darkness of the grave;
Thou, over whom thy immortality
Broods like the day, a master o'er a slave,
A presence which is not to be put by;
Thou little child, yet glorious in the might
Of heaven-born freedom on thy being's height...

(1948, 233)

Note especially this line: "Some fragment of his dream of human life." That is what the child creates in his playing. His play has the reality of dream, and he responds to it as we have seen the dream ego respond within the dream: that is, with complete openness. There is response, but no consciousness of response, no analogue I. The child creates a narrative and lives in it at the same time.

Note, too, the situation. Mother and father look on lovingly, acceptingly, providing unconditional positive regard. The bicameral child flourishes in such an environment because incomprehensible demands are not being made from the outside. I have indicated that this was my situation in my family's house on Long Island Sound. Stress brings on the outside world too soon, stunting the work of imagination. Wordsworth describes a well-situated child.

Those fragments from the child's dream of human life are absolutely real to him, just as the sleeping giant was. The child's world is inhabited by many such fragments. That is why the poet says the child

... dost keep
Thy heritage, thou eye amongst the blind,
That, deaf and silent, read'st the eternal deep....

(1948, 110–112)

That "heritage" I take to be the archetypal ground. It is what has always been there; it is the eternal deep, with the word "deep" echoing the metaphorical placement of the unconscious as underground or under water. Ironically, consciousness itself gets in the way of our ability to be in touch with the archetypes. The *child* is "mighty prophet! Seer blest! / On whom those truths do rest," but, in stark and painful contrast, those truths are, for us, truths "which we are toiling all our lives to find, / In darkness lost..." This is why we are nostalgic for our bicameral childhood. Frightening it may have been, but it was magical, too. For this reason I want to amplify the whole idea of the bicameral mind.

Specifically, what might it be like to live in a bicamerally organized society? Here is a tourist in Egypt, writing to her parents in England in 1849:

> From the terrace of the mosque is what I should imagine the finest view in the whole world. Cairo, which is immense, lies at the feet, a forest of minarets and domes and towers. The Nile flows his solemn course beyond, the waters being still out (it is now high Nile), and the three Pyramids stand sharp against the sky. Here Osiris and his worshipers lived; here Aristotle came; here, later, Mahomet learnt the best of his religion and studied Christianity; here, perhaps, our Savior's mother brought her little son to open his eyes to the light. They are all gone ... but the Nile flows and the Pyramids stand there still. (1987, 33)

Thus Florence Nightingale wrote home. She captured what is eerily true about Egypt: something about it goes on, keeps going on, is paradoxically eternally present. I believe ancient Egypt to be the finest example of a fully developed (that is, aesthetically and philosophically complete) bicameral civilization that the world has ever known. It therefore serves my purpose here, which is to grasp what the bicameral mind is like for the person who lives in that way, and only in that way, for the entire span of life. For the person, in other words, who is living the way the child lives before consciousness develops, before consciousness makes him start to resemble everyone else. Or before consciousness makes it possible for him to live in the world as now it is—all three of these being possible, in turn, or even all at once.

The dream of the boat/streetcar, cited in the previous chapter, contains, I believe, a subtle reference to Egypt. The dream ego, you will recall, finds himself beside "a stream or canal" and an unusual craft into which he steps. I now add the fact that the dreamer is a man in his middle seventies, retired, and beginning a "new life" free of his former work-driven obligations. He is in a new place in his life, but it is also a place that may involve the crossing of a river. We are thus in the presence of a ubiquitous archetypal image, the river that separates this life and the afterlife. For our culture, perhaps, the Styx; for the Egyptians, obviously, the Nile. The east was for them, and always is, the place of dawn, of life; the west, the place of sunset, of darkness and death. This is by no means explicit in the dream. It is more a feeling, the sort of feeling that might lead a psychoanalytic conversation in the direction of these deep matters. The dream ego is open to this nuance, too, more than the conscious ego is. Death is not to be overly dwelt upon if one is to remain equanimously in the world of the living. But here it is, subtly, and with a suggestion of an Egyptian geography. For this dreamer it is an appropriate, if still somewhat distant, concern. The dream gives him (that is, his conscious ego) permission to ponder it. The sensibility of ancient Egypt does the same thing. We have already noted that, for the Egyptian, the dream is *seen,* not "had." This parallel wants further amplification.

James H. Breasted was, in his day, the foremost American Egyptologist; his *History of Egypt* (1912) remains a monument both to historiography and to his own sensibility. To scholarship and archaeology he added, subtly and indirectly, the stern but profound Congregational training he had received from the Chicago Theological Seminary. The same may be said of his *Development of Religion and Thought in Ancient Egypt* (1972; first published 1912). It was the Seminary, through its recognition of Breasted's remarkable talent for the acquisition of Hebrew, that turned him toward what was in that time the highly unusual and specialized field of Egyptology. Here is Breasted, from the latter book:

> We shall discern the emergence of the earliest abstract term known in the history of thought as moral ideas appear among the men of the Pyramid Age in the first half of the third millennium B.C.... As the earliest chapter in the intellectual history of man, its introductory phases are, nevertheless, of more importance than their intrinsic value as thought would otherwise possess, while the climax of the development is vital with human interest and human appeal....
>
> The all-enveloping power and glory of the Egyptian sun is the most insistent fact in the Nile valley, even at the present day as the modern tourist views him for the first time. The Egyptian saw him in different, doubtless original forms. At Edfu he appeared as a falcon, for the lofty flight of this bird, which seemed a very comrade of the sun, had led the early fancy of the Nile peasant to believe that the sun must be such a falcon, taking his daily flight across the heavens, and the sun-disk with the outspread wings of the falcon became the commonest symbol of Egyptian religion. As falcon he bore the name of Hor (Horus or Horos), or Harakhte, which means "Horus of the horizon." (1972, 8–9)

There is no difference between seeing the sun as a falcon and seeing the sleeping giant. It is revealing that Breasted himself falls insensibly into the bicameral way of experiencing the world: he does not say that the sun was imagined as a falcon, for that would be to invoke consciousness. No; rather, he says, the sun *appeared* as a falcon. Of course he recovers quickly, and adds that the "early fancy of the Nile peasant" *believed* that "the sun must be such a falcon." Never mind; for a moment there he was one with his subject.

Now, what Breasted felt to be the "climax of the development [of the intellectual history of man]" was the short, idiosyncratic championing of monotheism (as Breasted saw it) by the heretic pharaoh Ikhnaton (Breasted's transliteration). Here is a bit of Breasted's introduction to his translation of one of that king's hymns to his sun-god:

> [The] hymns ... afford us a glimpse into the new world of thought, in which we behold this young king and his associates lifting up their eyes and attempting to discern God in the illimitable sweep of his power—God no longer of the Nile valley only, but of all men and of all the world. (1972, 323–324)

Heady stuff. My point in citing this is to show that there was, for Breasted, a conflation of bicamerality (which he tacitly acknowledges) with belief, in the usual, modern sense of that word, which equates belief with consciousness. This conflation persists. Because of it, there is much difficulty for today's student of ancient Egypt trying to grasp what the psyche of the ancient Egyptian person was really like. A further difficulty arises from the fact that most people who inquire into this problem are dependent on translations of hieroglyphic texts, and we have no way of "checking out" the accuracy of those translations, let alone their probable bias in favor of either bicamerality or consciousness. Here, for example, are two versions of the same passage from the beginning of a Middle Kingdom text, usually given a title such as "The Dialogue of the World-weary Man with his Soul":

(1) Don't go my soul!
   Stay!
   Only with me will thou arise! (Reed, 1978, 17)

(2) Let not my soul go away; it should wait for me because of
      me.
   Let my soul not depart, that it may attend to it for me.
   Let not my *ba* go away, but it shall respect me instead...
                    (The Oriental Institute, University of Chicago;
                                        undated mimeograph)

I cite these passages to make the point that it is a questionable proce-dure to argue for a theory of mind from translations of hieroglyphics. What is a legitimate procedure for a poem of Wordsworth or Donald Hall may not help us with a translation of an Egyptian text. However, Szpakowska's observation, cited above, about the Egyptian expres-sion of *seeing*, rather than *having* the dream, is not problematic in this way; it is completely straightforward and unambiguous.

There is other evidence that embodies what the bicameral world of Egypt was like. Consider, first, the building of the great pyramids at Gizeh. These incredible monuments were not built with what we now think of as slave labor. Rather, the labor force—some ten thou-sand people at the site in any given year—worked voluntarily, was well taken care of, housed and fed and the sick tended. Here is one description:

> The great enterprise of the Fourth Dynasty [the Gizeh pyr-amids] most probably rested on national service or "corvee" labor, not on slavery. In Egypt slaves were an expensive and somewhat irrelevant luxury, because the Nile valley supported such a large population...the crushing magnitude of pyramid building can scarcely have escaped a cost in human life, any more than the great building projects of our own time....

> Khufu left posterity a unique image of unrivaled scope, syn-onymous at once with an inhuman scale of power and a super-human if not divine level of technical accomplishment.... The Great Pyramid bore the Egyptian name Akhet-Khufu "horizon of Khufu,," the place where the king would rise as certainly as the sun rises over the eastern desert mountains every morning. King and sun-god are now one... (Forman and Quirke, 1996, 47–48)

Why, it is fair to ask, would so many people willingly do such fantastically difficult work, year after year? Because, I suggest, they were hearing, bicamerally, the voice of the god-king exhorting them to fulfill their own destiny, which was to have a role in preserving, forever, the ordered universe, the universe dependent upon, *entirely* dependent upon, the sun. And the king and the sun are one. The king is the earthly incarnation of Horus, son of Isis and Osiris; the Horus-king, at his death, *becomes* an Osiris, lord of the underworld; and a new Horus-king reigns. Thus the king does not die, and the voice of the now-Osiris king (the former monarch) is heard throughout Egypt, always.

Try to imagine those ten thousand people at the construction site of the great pyramid of Khufu. They work with voices in their ears, voices that say they are contributing to the very order of the universe. It is an order they have experienced year after year, as the Nile flooded and nourished their land. It is an order that they have experienced as the stars passed overhead, season after season, one constellation following another forever. The pyramid, a mountain oriented by the four cardinal directions, is a part of that order, and so is every worker. If you seek evidence of the force of bicamerality, stand in awe not only of the pyramids, but of those who built them. Like Wordsworth's imagining child, they, too, felt watched over by parental divine presences. They, too, like the child, are participating in the creation of their world.

One more example of Egyptian bicamerality, and I am done. In the Egyptian texts known as *The Book of the Dead*, the scene of paramount importance is the depiction of the soul of the deceased, in the presence of Osiris, being weighed against the feather of truth. The feather stands for justice, order, piety, goodness, virtue. It is the instrument against which the soul is judged to be worthy of the pleasant and peaceful afterlife the Egyptians imagined—or to be devoured, forthwith, by a horrible mythical beast who lurks threateningly nearby. The feather is a representation of *Maat*, the Egyptian idea of order. Starting with the reign of Seti I we see in reliefs a scene, increasingly common, in which the king presents Maat to a god, such as Osiris. In general, the symbolism is that the offering of Maat by the king, as Emily Teeter writes, "invokes the king's sense of piety to the god, and perhaps a dedication of himself, symbolized by his name, and his efforts on behalf of the god" (1997, 92). We are seeing here another representation, it seems to me, of what the pyramid stood for: the preservation of order in the universe. While, as Teeter explains, the meaning of the ritual of the king's presentation of Maat to the god changed over time, the general principle remained steadfastly in place. "The ritual stressed [the king's] new relationship with Maat and his commitment to the gods.... [T]he ritual may be viewed as a symbol of confidence, of a new direct association with the world of the gods" (1997, 93). Maat is not an idea, or a principle. It is a thing. It can be held in the hand. It can be presented. It is real in the same way that the sleeping giant is real, or Wordsworth's child's "little plan or chart." It does not "stand for" something; it *is* something. The Egyptians were masters at making concrete realities out of what would be for us abstract ideas. For light, the king; for order, a feather. This concreteness is how the bicameral mind takes in all experience: the sun *is* the king, and vice versa. For Wordsworth's child, his "wedding or a festival" *is* a wedding or a festival. There is no idea of metaphor, or "imagination," or "belief." The child, in play, creates reality. 'Tis a consummation devoutly to be wished. At least it was surely a wish I held on to, long after my once-bicameral childhood had been covered over by school and custom. Here are two examples.

In 1945, when I was eleven years old, my mother and I were living in New York City. My father had gone off to Great Britain, to serve with the Eighth Air Force in the Second World War. I was still quite happily on my own much of the time, although a kind and generous first cousin (the child that my mother's sister had been pregnant with that summer of 1933 in Old Black Point) made my transfer to a new school a happy experience, and we lived only a few blocks from the Metropolitan Museum of Art. Almost every weekend during the school year I would walk there, on my own, and visit the Egyptian Wing of that wonderful museum. I now know, of course, that my fascination with Egypt was grounded in its answer to the question of what happens after death, as I said in Chapter Two; but of course I had no idea, when I was eleven, that I was in thrall to an unconscious presence. Indeed, late one Saturday afternoon I was among the mummies (they were downstairs, where the Costume Institute is now), looking closely at the representations of the goddess Nut, the god Geb, and Osiris and Isis, as they were to be found inside wooden coffins that were on display in long rows. Absorbed as I was, I didn't hear the announcement that the museum was closing, and not until some of the lights were turned out did I realize what was happening. I tried to leave, but the iron gate across the exit from the mummies had already been locked. So there I was, among the mummies. It occurred to me, momentarily, that I could just spend the night. I would keep quiet, the place would be thrilling, and I could stroll out with the crowd the next morning. But I soon realized that my mother might wonder what had become of me, so I called out, and a very disgruntled guard unlocked the gate. I still like to imagine, though, what that night in the Egyptian Wing would have been like.

Fast forward, to 1981. My daughter Helen and I were in Egypt, touring the pharaonic monuments. Anwar Sadat had just been assassinated, so fear kept most tourists away; we had the sites pretty much to ourselves. We entered the pyramid of Unas at Sakkara, and its burial chamber (excellent photographs of which may be found in Forman and Quirke [1996, 54–55]). The ceiling of this chamber is a rendition of a perfect night sky, a tent of schematic stars—indeed, lines of stars, arranged above the pharaoh's sarcophagus—and now above the visitor as well. I stood in that space and suddenly felt entirely at peace with the idea of death, an afterlife, a translation of myself through time and space to, or through, those stars so wonderfully above me. It was a moment that stays with me. It was a bicameral sense of death, not conscious at all. I have indicated how fears of death accompanied my birth, and how my parents were frightened always because of it. But all of that is nothing but my conscious, rational analysis of what *also* remains a pure experience. It is this purity that makes the bicamerally perceived world so attractive. It is a wonder to not think, to just *be*, instead.

But, as Wordsworth so poignantly wrote, we grow away from all of that:

> Shades of the prison-house begin to close
> Upon the growing boy,
> But he beholds the light, and whence it flows,
> He sees it in his joy;
> The youth, who daily farther from the east
> Must travel, still is Nature's priest,
> And by the vision splendid
> Is on his way attended;
> At length the man perceives it die away
> And fade into the light of common day.
> (1948, 232, lines 67–76)

And so it does. But the progression is slow. The child, oscillating between bicamerality and consciousness, holds these opposites in one encompassing mind. It is this that makes the child the "best philosopher." But it becomes harder and harder to do. The sleeping giant will inexorably become a mundane hill in the distance, and will remain so as long as we are obligated to live in what people call "the real world." The consequences of living in that reality are the subject of the next chapter. But one more principle is at work in my own story.

I am, as I have said, an introverted person. It was natural for me to turn my attention inward, to dwell within my own images and fantasies. I really did think first of spending the night alone with the mummies, rather than rejoining the populated ordinary world. But introversion is not the prevailing mode of being in the United States today: only twenty percent of the population of this country is introverted. Certainly, during my growing up, there were few kindred souls to be found, and I did feel, from time to time, as if my extroverted schoolmates and cousins and friends in Old Black Point were somehow more polished, more at ease, and were having more fun with games and parties than I was with my mineral collection or my microscope. But I was never really upset by any of this, and my parents never pressed me to be different, or to be more like them, a fact for which, as I have said, I am still grateful. I bring this up again to make a point: this is an *introvert's book*. My choice of Hamlet and J. Alfred Prufrock as primary examples of adolescence and early adulthood are choices driven by my identification with these two introverted characters. I know, as anyone trained in analysis knows, that there is no judgment to be made about introversion versus extroversion. They have equal value and equal force, positive or negative, ego or shadow, in every person. I write out of introversion because it is what I have known. It has led me to choose Hamlet and Prufrock to be in this book, and it has had its effects on love, marriage, my children, and my sense of how my world works.

If, reader, some of this feels unfamiliar to you, perhaps you are extroverted; if so, my introversion will be an aspect of your shadow. So be it; it is always useful to try to imagine how another type lives. If you are an introvert, you may be too at ease with me. If so, step back and reflect about how an extrovert might view things. The ability to "imagine the Other" is rare in a world dominated by electronic imagery and a common culture of pop icons and consumerism. These are forces that shape conformity to a group. Extroverts are comfortable in groups; introverts are not. An extroverted child will become conscious of other people and the outer world. An introverted child's consciousness is directed inward. Each sometimes fears and sometimes envies the other. But it is consciousness itself that is the achievement of childhood. The next task is that of constructing an identity. That task is at hand when questions like "Who shall I be in the world?" and "How do I want to be seen by others?" begin to grow in the mind. These questions are very much a part of adolescence, to which we now turn. In childhood, consciousness is created. One challenge of adolescence is what to do with it.

CHAPTER 4

ADOLESCENCE
OBSTINATE QUESTIONINGS

HERE IS ADOLESCENCE, described in the "Intimations" ode by the poet looking back on it:

> The thought of our past years in me doth breed
> Perpetual benediction: not indeed
> For that which is most worthy to be blest;
> Delight and liberty, the simple creed
> Of childhood, whether busy or at rest,
> With new-fledged hope still fluttering in his breast:—
> Not for these I raise
> The song of thanks and praise;
> But for those obstinate questionings
> Of sense and outward things,
> Fallings from us, vanishings;
> Blank misgivings of a creature
> Moving about in worlds not realized,
> High instincts before which our mortal nature
> Did tremble like a guilty thing surprised:
> But for those first affections,
> Those shadowy recollections,
> Which, be they what they may,
> Are yet the fountain-light of all our day,
> Are yet a master-light of all our seeing:
> Uphold us, cherish, and have power to make
> Our noisy years seem moments in the being
> Of the eternal silence: truths that wake,
> To perish never...

(1948, 233)

We have, in the poem, come away from the exhilaration of child-hood; the tone is entirely different. So it is with the onset of adolescence. "A creature / Moving about in worlds not realized" is a good description of a person in this most complicated and difficult time of life. The world of childhood is over, but the world of adulthood has not begun. And yet, in order to consider adolescence at all, it is necessary to take account of how the adult world *is*, which is one thing, and how that world is *understood to be* by the young person about to enter it, which is an entirely different thing. In considering infancy and childhood, it was possible to think of them as isolated ways of being in the world, and we have done so in the two previous chapters. This cannot be done in considering adolescence, because the adolescent is both isolated from and connected to the larger world. For the adolescent, the adult world is necessary and appalling at once. Hence the power and ubiquitousness of the collective "youth culture." Adults encountering the culture of youth often feel themselves assaulted by a crazed, cacophonous mass, in which no one seems to have individual and particular thoughts and feelings. Even a momentary individual estrangement—moving to a new school, say—can make a teenager, previously so embedded in the collective, feel unbearably lonely.

On top of this, one of the most painful aspects of middle school and high school is the sharp, inflexible division of students by themselves into groups of their own invention: athletes and cheerleaders—the popular ones—contrasted, often cruelly, with the nerds, isolates, and "losers" of various kinds. These divisions are reinforced by the whole culture of adolescence as it is found in magazines and television and, now, the internet. This culture is a world few adults ever even venture near, let alone come to understand. Adults basically mistrust adolescents because so much of what they do is foreign and baffling. And adolescents feel the same way about adults: not that they are baffling, but that they "just don't get it." Again, we must now look at two worlds at once.

It was often said during the ecstatic, troubled and rebellious decade of the 1960s, at least in the United States and Western Europe, that the youth had developed and were living in an entirely separate culture. It was this culture that made schooling irrelevant, that created completely new music, celebrating drugs and sexuality and what Marshall McLuhan called "cool" media: media that appealed to more than one sense, that were ambiguous visually and verbally, and therefore profoundly, seductively engaging (1965, 22). "Cool" media like television were seen as opposed to the "hot" medium of print. Print, with its clarity and linearity and slow, cumulative development of logic-based argument, seemed hopelessly distant and cerebral. This separate culture of youth was a wholly new creation in the history of human experience. It changed adolescence from a period of apprenticeship to a world all its own. The "hot" adult world was rejected, and the "cool" (in McLuhan's sense) world of the youth culture superseded it. In 1970, I wrote, of McLuhan's idea, that

> [t]he paradox is that a medium which is clear and unambiguous is *less* involving than one which is unclear.... McLuhan's idea.... flies in the face of common sense. Common sense says that clarity is a prerequisite for involvement. A little reflection, however, reveals that this proposition is at least over-simple. Thus, it is reasonably clear that many early civilizations tended to be most concerned with those elements in their experience that were least clear: for example, the overwhelming concern of the dynastic Egyptian civilization was not this world but, rather, the afterlife.... But, as "understanding" increases, involvement decreases, and what were once intense preoccupations become perfunctory gestures....
>
> [I]t may be useful to adduce a few less exotic examples of the relationship between the "temperature" of a medium and the degree of involvement it engenders....
>
> The music that students find involving ... provides a striking example of a cool medium. The names of performing groups are often puzzling or indeed oxymoronic: the Stone Balloon, the Who, Jefferson Airplane. Compare "the Andrews Sisters," a name perfectly suited to the hot [single-sense] medium of

radio. The same coolness pervades song titles: "The Sound of Silence"; "New Christ Cardiac Hero"; "My Uncle Used to Love Me But She Died." Compare "Summertime"; "When You Wore a Tulip"; "Tea for Two"; "Some Enchanted Evening." The [new] song is … not in print (that is, not linear) at all; it is, instead, a total *field*, made of sound and effect, rather than sound and sense. (119–121)

I propose that today's adolescent is living within a "total field" of his or her own creation. In 1970 I saw this as a profound cultural phenomenon, one that (among other things) rendered "hot" schooling at least suspect and at most irrelevant for the students subjected to it. That feeling of irrelevance is often still a hallmark of the adolescent view of school and of older people in general. But it is not simply media-driven, as I once supposed. It is a defining attribute of adolescence, and it has been with us for a very long time. It is this that leads me to use, as my example of an adolescent in the adult world, Prince Hamlet himself. Those "blank misgivings" of Wordsworth are Hamlet's, too, and they have an archetypal foundation.

First, though, why Hamlet? He is usually understood as a preternaturally articulate and sensitive young adult who is caught up in a tragic situation not of his own making. I have no quarrel with this reading. But here I wish to emphasize the adolescent aspects of Hamlet's situation. By so doing we gain the advantage of being able to look at this time of life through the eyes of a person more articulate than any real-life adolescent. Some of the adolescent characteristics of Hamlet's life are:

- he is mistrustful of all adults, including his mother, his uncle, and his own father, both as ghost and memory;
- he is in the throes of anguished love for Ophelia;
- but she and her brother Laertes are part of the corrupt court;
- he has only one trustworthy ally his own age, his friend Horatio, but Horatio has no standing in the court;

- he feels he has to create a false self, a trickster (his "madness"), in order to hide his true self from the adults around him;
- this false self is interpreted as mad by the adults and it makes them upset and angry;
- he feels he must take on the whole unjust world all by himself, but at the same time is in awe of the task before him ("The time is out of joint. O cursed spite that ever I was born to set it right!");
- he is by turns suicidal ("To be or not to be"), irrationally impulsive (his murder of Polonius, for example), horribly funny (as in what he says about his father's funeral followed immediately by his mother's wedding: "Thrift, thrift, Horatio: the funeral baked meats / did coldly furnish forth the marriage tables"; of the body of Polonius: "I'll lug the guts into the neighbor room"), and bawdy ("That's a fair thought to lie between maids' legs").

He is, in short, puzzled and troubled by a host of adolescent concerns. In his world things are not clear until, at the very end, Laertes spells it out: "The King, the King's to blame." Only then can Hamlet, dying, bring order and justice to the world around him by acting unambiguously as himself. Up until this moment, he has been conflicted, and these conflicts have rendered him by turns helpless and resolute, impulsive and suicidal, comic and desperate; in short, he lives, until the very end of the play, within the waves of conflicting emotions. It is this oscillation between two opposed states, two opposed ways of being, that characterizes adolescence. On the one hand, the adolescent is dependent, unformed, and not yet in the world; on the other hand, that same adolescent is (or wants to appear) independent, worldly, and complete. The same person holds both these views at the same time. One reason parents are so often puzzled by their adolescent children is that they cannot know which of these two people is going to show up at any given moment. In more general terms, we may return to the dichotomies presented in Chapter One of this book; the adolescent may be hero or victim, sometimes from one moment to the next. And the adolescent may view the world as orderly one minute and chaotic the next. But if it is hard to be around such a person, it is even harder to *be* such a person. In the 1960s, the social satirists who called themselves the Firesign Theater asked a question that captures the problem: "How can you be in two places at once if you're not anywhere at all?" Now, *that* is an obstinate question. Humorless Wordsworth would not have phrased it thus, alas, but the import of the question was apparent to him. The two places were, and are, hero/victim in one's inner life, and the outer world as orderly or chaotic. The adolescent is quite literally in between, all the time. The concept of being in between is the concept of liminality, as originated in the work of A. van Gennep on rites of passage (1960) and described by Victor W. Turner:

> The neophyte may be buried, forced to lie motionless in the posture and direction of customary burial, may be stained black, or may be forced to live for a while in the company of masked and monstrous mummers representing, *inter alia,* the dead, or, worse, the un-dead. The metaphor of dissolution is often applied to neophytes....
>
> The other aspect, that they are not yet classified [as either children or adults], is often expressed in symbols modeled on processes of gestation and parturition. The neophytes are likened to or treated as embryos, newborn infants, or sucklings by symbolic means which vary from culture to culture....
>
> The essential feature of these symbolizations is that the neophytes are neither living nor dead from one aspect, both living and dead from another. Their condition is one of ambiguity and paradox, a confusion of all the customary categories. Liminality may perhaps be regarded as the Nay to all positive structural assertions, but also in some sense the source of them all, and, more than that, a realm of pure possibility whence novel configurations of ideas and new relations may arise....

We are not dealing with structural contradictions when we discuss liminality, but with the essentially unstructured (which is at once destructured and prestructured) and often the people themselves see this in terms of bringing neophytes into close connection with the deity and supernatural power. (1967, 95–96)

The anthropologist has the advantage, here, of studying cultures in which liminality is recognized and celebrated for what it is in the lives of initiates. Our more advanced society has lost touch with the necessity of such recognition. Adults—parents especially—are fundamentally conflicted about adolescents: either they want them to grow up, or they want them to stay children. This conflict is of course mirrored in, and by, adolescents themselves.

I propose that the archetype of adolescence is the archetype of liminality itself: the state of being in transition, from one known place—childhood—to another, adulthood. The cultural and psychological problem here is that we do not have a fixed archetypal image, or figure, or symbol, to represent this transitory, impermanent, fluid, state. The closest representation is Hermes, Mercury, and adolescence is mercurial—an image to which we shall return. Let us see what we can make of the problem presented by a fluid, mutable image.

Here, Heinz Kohut is helpful. Kohut posits that every person has two fundamental needs: one is to be mirrored—that is, truly seen; the other is to have another person to idealize, to grow toward. Without mirroring, one does not exist; without idealizing, one has no goal (1985, 79). I "solved" this problem for myself by ignoring (really, repressing) my parents' preoccupation with their own lives and their consequent neglect of mine, while at the same time creating a questing and engaged private self, a sort of miniature adult, who could read or look at the moon with a telescope, unbothered by anything personal in his outside world and feeling superior to it. Thus I both mirrored myself and idealized myself. Only years later, in analysis, did I touch the pain of this isolation, and the buried anger that came along with my feeling that I had to minister to myself. Only then did I come to understand why the character of Hamlet has drawn me to him for so long, and why it was important for me to teach the play *to* adolescents to show them that it was *about* adolescents (Hamlet and Ophelia), as I am suggesting here. It is Hamlet alone who intuits what adults are supposed to do, and therefore knows how profoundly all of the adults around him—his mother, Claudius, and Polonius—have failed. On my own tiny stage, I did the same.

Of Hamlet, Kohut writes,

> It is the idealized pole of Hamlet's self that has yet to be firmed and activated, and his bitterness and sarcastic pseudo-insanity on the way to this achievement are no more than the out-ward signs of the intense work that is going on in the depths. The ghost appears—he is still "outside"—but not as evidence of a static failure: he expresses the beginning of the work of integration of the self as all of Hamlet's inner resources are mobilized. Ophelia is rejected and abandoned to her death. This is cause for mourning and self-reproach from the side of Hamlet's guilty self. And yet the work must continue, what-ever the cost to self and others. The self objects (the mother and the father figures of Claudius–Polonius) are no help to Hamlet. They do not provide him with the idealizing figure he so desperately needs. They want social compliance and pre-tense of greatness and can promise only external success and high position. [How accurately this describes some parents of adolescents today!] Only the twinship support of Laertes [only at the very end] and the childhood memories of the sus-taining Yorick [and Horatio's constancy] are helpful. Hamlet must find psychological strength within himself and go on until it is completed. The ultimate deed, the killing of the guilty usurper of the throne of Denmark, is no more than the external symbol for the inner achievement: the idealized pole, weakly established because of paternal distance, has firmed the self. Adequate, if hasty, action has realized the program. Hamlet has found an ideal in which to believe, for which to

fight. The wrong has been put to right. Hamlet has found himself, and now may safely die. What the tragedy portrays is the regained ability of a self to run its course toward a fulfilled death. Great tragedy is the portrayal of the full course of life, however condensed into a narrow span of time and fitted into traditional scenes and acts. (1985, 77)

"It is the idealized pole of Hamlet's self that has yet to be firmed and activated..." This is a cause of Hamlet's state of liminality throughout almost the entire play. Hamlet's life before his father's murder, as far as we can tell—and there isn't much evidence—was conventional and featureless. Immediately after the ghost has told Hamlet to "remember me" and then disappeared into the coming dawn, Hamlet soliloquizes,

> Remember thee?
> Ay, thou poor ghost, while memory holds a seat
> In this distracted globe. Remember thee?
> Yea, from the table of my memory
> I'll wipe away all trivial fond records,
> All saws of books, all forms, all pressures past
> That youth and observation copied there....
> (1986, I, 5, lines 95–102)

That is a lot to get rid of, unless there wasn't a great deal anyway. Kohut suggests, I think accurately, that, until the very end of the play, there are no solid structures in Hamlet's psyche: the adolescent again. And just after his meeting with the ghost, Hamlet, as I have mentioned, says to Horatio and Marcellus and Bernardo:

> The time is out of joint. O cursed spite
> That ever I was born to set it right!
> (1986, I, 5, lines 189–190)

It is useful to try to imagine *whose* spite Hamlet has in mind here. In effect, he is asking why he, of all people, has been selected to put things right. Selected, we must add, by his father. This is nothing new from the point of view of the adolescent; many fathers, explicitly or implicitly, "select" futures for their sons. When I was a teenager I knew twin brothers, exactly my age. One day the two of them asked their father whether they could go, together, to whichever college they might select, when the time came. "Of course," said their father, "you may choose any college you want. But I'll pay your way to Yale."

Hamlet, here, feels he has been appointed to a task. Of course it is his father's ghost who has done the appointing, and that is what makes the word "spite" so interesting—so adolescent. As we know, there is a part of Hamlet that vows to carry out the work of revenge immediately. But there is another part that holds back, is blocked by scruple, or by timidity, or by ambivalence about his mother, or by abhorrence of violence, or by ... once again, the ebb and flow of opposites in the adolescent psyche. The essence of this inner "double view" of what he must do is captured precisely in this exchange between Hamlet and the ghost:

> **Ghost**: If thou didst ever thy dear father love—
> **Hamlet**: O God!
> **Ghost**: Revenge his foul and most unnatural murder.
> **Hamlet**: Murder?
> **Ghost**: Murder most foul, as in the best it is,
>   But this most foul, strange, and unnatural.
> **Hamlet**: Haste me to know 't, that I, with wings as swift
>   As meditation or the thoughts of love,
>   May sweep to my revenge. (1986, I, 5, lines 23–31)

How swift is this? "As meditation or the thoughts of love"— hardly metaphors for speed; rather, metaphors for deliberate pondering or a steady state of goodness—or whatever "love" may suggest. Think of any metaphor for speed and substitute it, and you will feel how ambivalent Hamlet reveals himself to be, even here, even before he hears who has done the murder.

A great advantage of using Hamlet as an example of the adolescent psyche is that Hamlet speaks in soliloquy. Consequently, we may be sure we are hearing him in his truest voice, unencumbered by any pressure to adapt to a particular listener or situation (Hamlet is a master of adaptability). It is rare for adults to hear adolescents express themselves in their truest voice; they are almost always hyperaware of their audience (this is one thing that makes psychotherapy with them difficult). Hamlet's most well-known soliloquy is, of course, the "To be or not to be" speech. I want to look at it in the light of an observation by Donald Meltzer and M. H. Williams:

> As mutes and audience we follow the hero, with a peculiar mixture of adulation and irritation, as he attempts to disentangle the riddle of his uncle-father's incestuous marriage and murder, from the mystery of the "undiscovered country" from which no traveler returns. This is ultimately his own inner self, whose image hovers always out of reach, sometimes glimpsed beyond the images of his mother or of Ophelia—yet, as with Orpheus and Eurydice, always frustrated or falsified by the unreal responses of others, whenever any potential pain of recognition or mutual understanding appears within reach. Time and again, attempts to pursue the developmental mode of "exploring the mystery" are converted, through an instantaneous switch of energies, into the essentially destructive and violent mental mode of "solving the riddle": not just by the visionless characters but also by the hero. And this contrast between two distinct mental modes which are operating in parallel—exploring the mystery and solving the riddle—is what constitutes the texture of the aesthetic conflict throughout the play. It accounts for the ambivalence of its fascination; and for the fact that the latent imagery of the play never reaches a conclusion or a solution. (1988, 85)

One of the literally fatal attractions of suicide, from the standpoint of the person contemplating it, is that it apparently both explores the mystery and solves the riddle. The riddle, for Hamlet, is the question he has already asked himself: Why is it that he has been chosen to make things right? And the mystery to be explored is the whole question of the nature of the world. Why do such things happen? What is the purpose of anything? At the simplest level, Hamlet would "solve the mystery" by killing Claudius, a deed which would put Hamlet, once the truth were known, on the "hero" end of our continuum; presumably, it would also restore order to the Danish court. (Whether it would actually do these things is problematical at best.) On the other hand, to explore the ultimate mystery means to find out what happens after death, and there is only one way to find that out. Is it better to "suffer the slings and arrows of outrageous fortune [that is, do nothing], or to take arms against a sea of troubles," or to commit suicide? And note again how Hamlet's choice of metaphor reveals his ambivalence: how could anyone take arms against a *sea* of anything? And—he goes on—suppose dying is a sleep? Well and good; but with sleep come dreams. In a larger sense, when we contemplate the afterlife, it is what we imagine that gives us pause. Thus a real deed—suicide—is undermined by thought itself. One domain of experience is in endless conflict with another: action versus thought, extroversion versus introversion, being still moving versus being still. It is this oscillation that the "To be or not to be" speech reflects. As is typical of Hamlet, he poses the question to himself, but he cannot answer it-yet. Neither can adolescents. They, like Hamlet, have to wait. That is what liminality is all about. Easy for us to say: we have been through it, and survived. Impossible for today's adolescents to accept, though. Being told to wait says, "You're not ready," and they will do anything to prove that false. In the meantime, what Harold Bloom writes of Hamlet applies to all adolescents:

> The poet Swinburne, a good Shakespearean critic, observed that "the signal characteristic of Hamlet's inner nature is by no means irresolution or hesitation or any form of weakness, but the strong conflux of contending forces." I think that is a clue to Hamlet's charisma.... Hamlet discovers that his life has been a quest with no object except his own endlessly burgeoning subjectivity. (2003, 98)

Adolescents do not "discover" this, of course. They just do it. As with Hamlet, the discovery comes later.

We can now contrast adolescence with childhood in a useful way. Childhood is about coming to consciousness, which happens as it happens, not individually, but—as Jaynes proposed—through inevitable encounters with an Other. The realization of consciousness is a profound breakthrough in our understanding of ourselves and the world, and once we achieve it we cannot go back. Adolescence is an entirely different matter. An adolescent can be an imitation adult one moment and a childlike creature the next. Thus adolescence has the shape-shifting of the trickster archetype about it, with which adolescence has plausibly been associated, as for example by Frankel. He writes,

> The Hermes/trickster archetype constellates in adolescence and is distinctly related to the manifestations of persona and shadow.... Hermes is known to show up whenever change is imminent. He is the mobile, volatile element in any transformation.... Hermes' nature is one of paradox: he is the god of communication as well as the patron saint of liars and god of merchants and thieves.... Given his changing and unstable nature, Hermes as quicksilver is in accord with our characterization of adolescence as a time of fluctuation in identity and character. (1998, 151)

There are many parallels between Hermes and the adolescent, and Frankel presents them to good effect; indeed, his book is one of the best treatments of adolescence. But to use Hermes himself as emblematic of adolescence is problematic. Not that Frankel does this. He says the Hermes archetype constellates in adolescence; he does not say Hermes *is* adolescence, but a reader used to equating the gods with archetypes might read past Frankel's actual way of putting it. That is why I bring the point up here. Hermes is *always* the trickster, *always* the god of borders, *always* liminal, and therefore always changing. Every other god and goddess is always what each one is, and only that. Aphrodite is always and only feminine eros, Marilyn Monroe; Artemis is always and only the huntress and radical virgin. Artemis will never love a man, and Aphrodite will never take up archery. Hephaistos is always craft, technology, the artisan; Ares is pure aggression, and so on. Hermes is not a permanent adolescent; there is no such thing, any more than a person can stay in liminal space for a lifetime. (The pathology of the *puer aeternus* looks like permanent liminality, but there is too much pain associated with for it to be a viable mode of being.) To assign such an archetype to adolescence is to miss the point: adolescence is, thank the gods, transitory exactly *because* it is liminal.

Even so, it has its eternally valuable aspect, as Wordsworth reminds us:

> But for those first affections
> Those shadowy recollections
> Which, be they what they may,
> Are yet the fountain-light of all our day,
> Are yet a master-light of all our seeing...
>
> (1948, 233)

It is these things for which he raises "[t]he song of thanks and praise." He is thankful for the other side of adolescence, those "first affections," representing an aspect of liminality to be treasured. I turn now to that.

Think of "first": the first being away from home, the first kiss, the first drive after getting the license, the first making love. Each of these represent threshold crossings, and each has an enormous energy charge associated with it because of that fact. Not only are the moments intense; they are also unique. They can happen only once. More of them occur in adolescence than at any other time. They have the initiatory quality that in earlier civilizations was contained in ritual, but in our modern, western world these rituals have faded away. But their psychic power remains. By moving initiation from a conscious ritual to an unconscious border-crossing, we have lost sight of a fundamentally important human experience. Even so, the numinosity of the crossing remains with us. It is this that accounts for the pain and the ecstasy we may feel when we remember our own adolescent life. Moments of crossing may look ahead in time, or they may look back. The driver's license, forward to a life of free choice and independence; the first kiss, back in time to a family connection free of conflict and trouble—an ideal connection, whatever the actual experience in the family may have been. Underneath such examples is another border, the permeable membrane that separates the unconscious from consciousness. In a continual state of becoming, the adolescent must also be in a continual state of negotiating the frontier between known and unknown. There is no more exciting place to be. This is the exhilaration of adolescence. In his book *Drumming at the Edge of Magic,* Mickey Hart, who was for more than twenty years the drummer for the Grateful Dead, describes an experience of this place:

> I practiced constantly, rarely playing in public aside from school band concerts. My most intense moments with the drum were private ones. I would sit with my drums and slowly begin warming the traps up, exciting the low end first, the bass drum, making it beat like a heart, slow and steady. The hi-hat would start clicking its metronomic click, and I'd start mixing in the middle voice, the rhythms of the snare drums and the tom-toms interweaving with the steady pulse of the bass. This interweaving of low end and middle is the main work of a traps drummer; at the high end, the shimmering harmonics of cymbals, bells, and gongs complete the drum voice.
>
> Ten minutes. Fifteen minutes. Twenty minutes. Then something curious would happen. I'd feel myself becoming lighter; I'd lose track of time. I realize now I was becoming entranced, but at the age of fifteen I had no idea what was going on. In my mind I connected it with an unusual experience that began when I was about five and that I associated, in

my adolescent mind, with my grandfather's stories. For years, just before sleep, bright undulating bubbles would slip under the door of my room and float toward me. They weren't menacing bubbles, although sometimes they bumped against me, covering my face. Their appearance was accompanied by a tingling sensation in the top of my nose. And each bubble had a specific sound, a kind of high-pitched hum.

Eventually I learned the secret of controlling these bubbles. I could make them advance and retreat, and sometimes I could even project myself up into them and gaze down on my body. Now I was getting the same feeling from my drumming. I never found it exhausting to drum for hours; it left me calm, energized, and grinning. (1990, 62)

We are here precisely on the border between conscious and unconscious. Those bubbles are the unconscious itself, seeping under the door and ready to take over, like sleep. And it is the very task of adolescence to gain some measure of control over them: in other words, to live deliberately on the border. The time will come, soon enough, when the conscious, outside world must take over and become the primary concern. But for now, in this liminal space, the two domains negotiate. Remember that in "To be or not to be," Hamlet describes, and feels, the dynamic of this negotiation. "To die, to sleep; / to sleep, perchance to dream...." To be here, or to be there. Like death, the unconscious, too, is an undiscovered country. All the more reason to be enthralled by it, to be attracted to it while at the same time being fearful.

Here are two examples of the enthralling quality of the border. Both are poems by Lawrence Ferlinghetti, from *A Coney Island of the Mind*:

> (1) That "sensual phosphorescence
>   my youth delighted in"
>   now lies almost behind me
>   like a land of dreams

wherein an angel
of hot sleep
dances like a diva
in strange veils
thru which desire
looks and cries
And still she dances
dances still
and still she comes
at me
with breathing breasts
and secret lips
and (ah)
bright eyes

(1958, 41)

(2) Peacocks walked
under the night trees
in the lost moon
light
when I went out
looking for love
that night
A ring dove cooed in a cove
A cloche tolled twice
once for the birth
and once for the death
of love
that night

(1958, 42)

This is the immediacy of adolescence. Will there be an end of it?
Inevitably. Adolescents grow up. Here is Hamlet, at the beginning of
his growing up. He is with his mother, after the tumultuous denoue-
ment of the play within the play (The "same lord" he refers to is
Polonius, whom he has just killed):

> Once more, good night,
> And when you are desirous to be blest,
> I'll blessing beg of you.—For this same lord,
> I do repent; but heaven hath pleased it so,
> To punish me with this, and this with me,
> That I must be their scourge and minister.
> I will bestow him and will answer well
> The death I gave him. So again, good night.
> I must be cruel only to be kind.
>
> (1986, III, 4, lines 154–162)

"Heaven hath pleased it so." This is not just an excuse; this is Hamlet understanding that he is in the toils of fate, that the universe contained, comprehended and imposed all that he had seen as his solely personal and therefore overwhelming burden. Hamlet now knows the source of the "spite" he has felt targeting him. It is not his father. It is "heaven," and heaven is not a mysterious "undiscovered country." It is a world with rules. Adolescence ends when that ordered world reasserts its presence. When it does, the threatening, puzzling, ecstatic condition of being on the border gives way to the constructed stability of adulthood.

Chapter 5

Early Adulthood
The Weight of Custom

Wordsworth's depiction of incipient adulthood is not one to encourage growing up. He sees it as an exercise in imitation:

> Then will he fit his tongue
> To dialogues of business, love, or strife;
> But it will not be long
> Ere this be thrown aside,
> And with new joy and pride
> The little actor cons another part;
> Filling from time to time his "humorous stage"
> With all the persons, down to palsied age,
> That life brings with her in her equipage;
> As if his whole vocation
> Were endless imitation.
>
> •
>
> Why with such earnest pains dost thou provoke
> The years to bring the inevitable yoke,
> Thus blindly with thy blessedness at strife?
> Full soon thy soul shall have her earthly freight,
> And custom lie about thee with a weight,
> Heavy as frost, and deep almost as life! (1948, 233)

The liminality of adolescence is a terrible but magical state. Custom kills it. Custom is how things are supposed to be, how things are done in the world of the adult. Whereas secondary schools must take into account the adolescence of their charges, graduation from those institutions means crossing over to a world where youth, no matter how insistently still a fact, is no longer regarded as an excuse. An eighteen-year-old with a job is supposed to be steady and reliable. A college freshman is supposed to have some sense of purpose in life. So the idea is to seem to be an adult, even when the inner life may be consumed by still-adolescent turmoil. This constructed adult now becomes the *persona,* at least in public, of the person who needs to appear to be grown up. It is a performance, to be sure, and it may change at any moment. But it is not unreal. It is a necessary construction—necessary for the purpose of fitting in. Our persona shows other people that we belong in their society. The archetypal foundation of the persona is the social contract, the set of customs and expectations that define a particular society in its time and place. The separate adolescent culture we examined in the previous chapter simply will not serve in the adult world, authentic though it was. So the stage of the "beginning adult" is a stage of becoming someone else, someone who can be seen as a plausible member of a larger but nonetheless cohesive group. The pressure to accomplish this exists whether a given individual succumbs to it or not.

There are two distortions of the persona to be aware of. One is the case when the persona is so much a conscious construction that it feels artificial, "phony," to the person who has constructed it. The other is where one is so identified with one's persona that it becomes all one has. There is no authentic person underneath, and the resulting inner turmoil is denied.

Then there are people who never seek to go along, or to get along. There are, for example, people who do not grow up, and hence never enter adult life. There are psychopaths, who are alienated from the collective. On the positive side, there are people whose genius, whose individuality, trumps collective ways of being. These, however, are exceptions. What of *ordinary* early adulthood? We focus here on persons whose constructed personas are more or less successful; they are, after all, the majority.

Now we turn away from our Wordsworthian foundation. Early adulthood is not, after all, his primary subject, which is his loss of, and then his reconnection to, the archetypal foundation of all experience. So my "case example" now becomes T.S. Eliot's poem *The Love Song of J. Alfred Prufrock.* I have already mentioned how this poem came into my life, and it is partly that experience I depend on for my explication of it. Prufrock himself is not presented to us as a young man; in fact, quite the opposite. He tells us "I grow old … I grow old … / I shall wear the bottoms of my trousers rolled." But Eliot wrote the poem when he was himself only twenty-three. Lyndall Gordon amplifies this point:

> Eliot said J. Alfred Prufrock was in part a man of about forty and in part himself. The demarcation between fiction and autobiography fits neatly along the lines of Prufrock's divided self. …
>
> Elements of Eliot are transformed into the lover—his shyness, his propriety of dress—but Eliot is more obviously aligned with Prufrock's other self, a solitary thinker who wishes to ask an "overwhelming question" and assault the genteel surfaces of Boston society with an apocalyptic truth. "Do I dare / Disturb the universe?" he wonders. … Prufrock's philosophic daring is continually checked by genteel scruples. (1998, 67)

Fiction and autobiography. There is a fictive element in the persona because it is more or less artfully, self-consciously constructed. But there is autobiography, too, because it is who we think we are, or who we feel we have to be, for others. Looking back, I can see that, in my adolescence, the persona I created was something of a struggle to maintain. It was imitative of my successfully social parents and of equally social contemporaries, schoolmates and others I had come to know in Old Black Point. But my preference was to be on my own. Hence there was always a hint of falseness in my "public" way of being. I was not aware of this falseness until I first read *Prufrock.* Under my relatively successful public performance was doubt, fed by my own overwhelming questions: What am I doing here? Wouldn't I be happier by myself? I did have one close friend, in school, who faced these questions, too, and we did talk, but the question remained.

Consider now the very beginning of Eliot's poem. The poem's narrator, Prufrock, and ourself, the reader, have evidently been conversing. That conversation has reached the point where Prufrock feels more or less comfortable about asking us to get up and walk with him on what will turn out to be a tour of the vicissitudes of his life. He does not know us well, for if he did, we would probably know him well, too, and the tour would be unnecessary; we would have done it already. "Let us go then, you and I," says Prufrock. I hear a tinge of exasperation in "then," as if we had talked long enough. Impatiently, he says, "Let us *go*, then."

But where? That question is deferred for the time it takes to answer, Go *when*? We go

> When the evening is spread out against the sky
> Like a patient etherised upon a table... (1936, 11)

What an extraordinary simile! It is of course Prufrock who sees the evening this way and, by telling us so, he takes us immediately into his imaginally constructed, subjective view of his world. Having been admitted to this domain, we are then led through streets and scenes that we, too, can see:

> Let us go, through certain half-deserted streets,
> The muttering retreats
> Of restless nights in one-night cheap hotels
> And sawdust restaurants with oyster-shells... (1936, 11)

This is familiar enough. But immediately we are drawn again into Prufrock's subjective self:

> Streets that follow like a tedious argument
> Of insidious intent
> To lead you to an overwhelming question...
> Oh, do not ask, "What is it?"

Let us go and make our visit.

—and then back to the outside world, but now a more sophisticated one:

> In the room the women come and go
> Talking of Michelangelo. (1936, 11)

This switching back and forth between the outer and the inner mirrors the psychological essence of early adulthood. The outer world is impersonal and full of expectations, while the inner world is idiosyncratic and unpredictable. Ordinarily, in the outer world, one does not announce that the evening looks like an anesthetized patient upon whom surgery is about to be performed. Why does Prufrock see the evening this way? Let us remember that the poem is a *love song*. Prufrock is taking us to a neighborhood where a certain kind of love is part of the setting: "... restless nights in one-night cheap hotels...." Looking back at his simile comparing the evening to a patient, it is clear that, for Prufrock, the evening is a time of artificial sleep, of not being able to feel, indeed of not being able to do anything; a time during which others will impersonally dissect inner spaces, possibly his own. Prufrock sees the evening in this startling way because he has, for the moment, projected a part of himself—the part that is diseased, passive, and helpless—onto the evening.

So from the very beginning of *Prufrock* we are made to oscillate between the inner world of the narrator and the outer world that we all live in. Prufrock then says, "Let us go and make our visit." But it is never clear whether this visit is to his world, or his mind, or to both at once. It is impossible to tell whether we are in the room with the women, or whether Prufrock simply knows how such women talk. Think of the ending of Beckett's *Waiting for Godot:*

Vladimir: Well? Shall we go?
Estragon: Yes, let's go.
> *They do not move.* (1976, Act 2)

To say, "Let us go, through certain half-deserted streets" is one thing; to actually *go* is quite another. This is an exact capturing of a core issue for early adulthood: there is the world of actual deeds, and there is the world of "perpetual possibility" (Eliot, 1943, 3). There is what one is doing, and there is what one imagines oneself doing. The fledgling associate in a law firm imagines herself a partner; the commuter on the bus imagines himself buying a new car; the newly married couple imagines the children to come, the larger house. Deeds and possibilities, realities and hopes emerge and retreat, one substituting for the other, in this stage of life.

To return to the text of the poem: the women talk about Michelangelo—chitchat about greatness. Meanwhile, Prufrock compares the yellow fog to a cat, echoing a poem of Carl Sandburg's. (The Eliot-based hit musical *Cats* is far in the future.) The cat is an animal, and alive, like the evening, but it, too, falls asleep, the natural counterpart of anesthesia. What are we to do with the animal side of our nature? Here it sleeps, away from those conversing women. It is a very large question in early adulthood. The desires are there, but so are custom and decorum—in contrast to adolescence. Within his love poem, Prufrock meditates on the problem of desire, but first he must face the general problem of how to be in the world. He is articulate, but puzzled and irresolute about almost everything except the "preparing" of a persona:

> And indeed there will be time
> For the yellow smoke that slides along the street,
> Rubbing its back upon the window-panes;
> There will be time, there will be time
> To prepare a face to meet the faces that you meet;
> There will be time to murder and create,
> And time for all the works and days of hands
> That lift and drop a question on your plate;
> Time for you and time for me
> And time yet for a hundred indecisions,

> And for a hundred visions and revisions,
>   Before the taking of a toast and tea. (1936, 12)

"[T]ime / To prepare a face to meet the faces that you meet" is the most straightforward portrayal of the construction of the persona that I have ever read. But it is the only straightforward statement here. Everything else is hedged around with contradiction. Notice how the uplifting thought of "visions" is immediately undercut by the prosaic "revisions." And notice, too, that a "question" is dropped on your plate, but we don't know what it is; and there will be time for all of this "before the taking of a toast and tea." And as if that weren't bad enough, we are next reminded that in the room the women are still talking about Michelangelo. No matter what Prufrock thinks or does, the world goes on, and there doesn't seem to be anything he can do about it. This is a key point: at the moment that the history of our life requires us to go out into the world, it can seem that our entry into the world will have no effect on it, *because to have an effect is to make changes, and change is anathema:*

> And indeed there will be time
> To wonder, "Do I dare?" and "Do I dare?"
> Time to turn back and descend the stair,
> With a bald spot in the middle of my hair—
> (They will say: "How his hair is growing thin!")
> My morning coat, my collar mounting firmly to the chin,
> My necktie rich and modest, but asserted by a simple pin–
> (They will say: "But how his arms and legs are thin!")
> Do I dare
> Disturb the universe?
> In a minute there is time
> For decisions and revisions which a minute will reverse.
>   (1936, 13)

Poor Prufrock! He has been going up the stair, a conventional metaphor for "rising" in the world, but now he sees that there will be time to turn around, to give it up. But if he does this he will reveal his bald spot: he will be gently ridiculed. So, indeed, does he dare? It does not seem so. To disturb the universe is just too much to take on, even if the universe consists only of women talking of Michelangelo. We shall return to the problem of women shortly. For now, there is the problem of repudiating the very world that has surrounded and protected him:

> For I have known them all already, known them all—
> Have known the evenings, mornings, afternoons,
> I have measured out my life with coffee spoons;
> I know the voices dying with a dying fall
> Beneath the music from a farther room.
> So how should I presume? (1936, 13)

The fact is, he cannot presume. At this point, he is caught between the nether millstone of the archetypal urge to find individual meaning and the greater millstone of custom. Custom is on top. Even so, though, there is the stirring of an idea about what is needed to escape:

> And I have known the eyes already, known them all—
> The eyes that fix you in a formulated phrase,
> And when I am formulated, sprawling on a pin,
> When I am pinned and wriggling on the wall,
> Then how should I begin
> To spit out all the butt-ends of my days and ways?
> And how should I presume? (1936, 14)

Having been "formulated," how can he now change? He has been classified, like an insect in a collection, complete with pin and label, except that he has been pinned alive. Here is the danger of the persona that works. It is completely understandable, predictable, and, above all, known to everyone. How, then, to shed it? And for what? To do so is to spit out, as he says, all the butt-ends of his days and ways; more generally, how can he "spit out" everything that is already left over, the waste represented by the events and accumulations of a life?

And there is an even harder problem, previously hinted at and to which he now turns: the problem of the women; really, it is the problem of sexuality, of the animal part of his nature that his society so conspires to bury.

> And I have known the arms already, known them all—
> Arms that are braceleted and white and bare
> (But in the lamplight, downed with light brown hair!)
> Is it perfume from a dress
> That makes me so digress?
> Arms that lie along a table, or wrap about a shawl.
> And should I then presume?
> And how should I begin? (1936, 14)

The fact is, he has no plausible way of beginning. These people, as we shall shortly see, will not hear him no matter what he says, and they will not pay attention, no matter what he does:

> Shall I say, I have gone at dusk through narrow streets
> And watched the smoke that rises from the pipes
> Of lonely men in shirt-sleeves, leaning out of windows?
>   (1936, 14)

This may be the neighborhood he has taken us to, but we are the reader, a stranger. His own society won't understand, and he despairs:

> I should have been a pair of ragged claws
> Scuttling across the floors of silent seas. (1936, 14)

A primitive animal, and not even the whole crab. Just claws, under the sea, primitive, instinctual, unconscious. And only "scuttling," with no direction or purpose.

But life goes on. Alas, the people around Prufrock are relentless in ignoring him, and this is partly his own fault. He is, quite naturally, afraid of his own passivity and the triviality of his existence, and this is subtly communicated to the people around him:

> And the afternoon, the evening, sleeps so peacefully!
> Smoothed by long fingers,
> Asleep ... tired ... or it malingers,
> Stretched on the floor, here beside you and me.
> Should I, after tea and cakes and ices,
> Have the strength to force the moment to its crisis?
> But though I have wept and fasted, wept and prayed,
> Though I have seen my head (grown slightly bald) brought
>   in upon a platter,
> I am no prophet—and here's no great matter;
> I have seen the moment of my greatness flicker,
> And I have seen the eternal Footman hold my coat, and
>   snicker,
> And in short, I was afraid. (1936, 14–15)

John the Baptist is hinted at, and this supplies an instance of triumph, of crisis, a life lived fully, and then a shocking death. But, as Prufrock concedes, *he* is no prophet. The moment of his greatness was not seized. The eternal Footman, knowing this, snickers.

And not only has Prufrock himself missed his moment. What is perhaps worse, the people around him have no conception of what it might mean to miss one's moment. Their lives are too conventional, too dissolved in the warm water of custom, to notice anything at all:

> And would it have been worth it, after all,
> After the cups, the marmalade, the tea,
> Among the porcelain, among some talk of you and me,
> Would it have been worth while,
> To have bitten off the matter with a smile,
> To have squeezed the universe into a ball
> To roll it toward some overwhelming question,
> To say, "I am Lazarus, come from the dead,
> Come back to tell you all, I shall tell you all"—

If one, settling a pillow by her head,
Should say: "That is not what I meant at all.
That is not it, at all." (1936, 15)

Even if he were to come back from the dead, it would not matter. Prufrock is a man who cannot, it seems, meet the challenge of early adulthood: he does not know how to *act* to make himself matter in the world he must live in.

But there is another way to try to matter. He can reveal himself totally and unflinchingly. Let us see what Prufrock makes of this idea.

It is impossible to say just what I mean!
But as if a magic lantern threw the nerves [*his* nerves!] in
    patterns on a screen:
Would it have been worth while
If one, settling a pillow or throwing off a shawl,
And turning toward the window, should say:
"That is not it at all,
That is not what I meant, at all." (1936, 15–16)

In other words, even if he were to reveal his innermost life, it would be dismissed, dissolved in the narcissism of one of those unreflective women.

Stalemated, Prufrock essentially confesses to us his profound sense of helplessness. He cannot solve the problem of becoming an individual while at the same time being beholden to the only society, the only collective, that he has known:

No! I am not Prince Hamlet, nor was meant to be;
Am an attendant lord, one that will do
To swell a progress, start a scene or two,
Advise the prince; no doubt, an easy tool,
Deferential, glad to be of use,
Politic, cautious, and meticulous;

Full of high sentence, but a bit obtuse;
At times, indeed, almost ridiculous—
Almost, at times, the Fool. (1936, 16–17)

He is not Hamlet, but he is not quite Polonius either, though he sees himself as leaning slightly in that direction. It is a sad conclusion about the society that surrounds him, and a sad conclusion about himself. There is one thing left for him to do, though. He can face his situation, by himself, with objectivity, with the understanding that comes from having been so caught by custom for so long. And this he does, with admirable and poignant clarity:

I grow old ... I grow old ...
I shall wear the bottoms of my trousers rolled.

Shall I part my hair behind? Do I dare to eat a peach?
I shall wear white flannel trousers, and walk upon the beach.
I have heard the mermaids singing, each to each.

I do not think that they will sing to me.

I have seen them riding seaward on the waves
Combing the white hair of the waves blown back
When the wind blows the water white and black. (1936, 17)

The mermaids will not sing to him. They will not include him either, but at least he has seen them, and he is willing to tell us so. Perhaps we, in contrast to those women he has known, will listen. Perhaps we sense that to see the mermaid is to see an image that ties together water and land, animal and human, body and mind, instinct and reflection. One escape from custom and form lies through the discovery of unexpected images of any sort: the evening like a patient etherized; the mermaids. The larger society may remain insensitive, callous, cut-off, smug, superior; but, with any good fortune at all, a unique—that is to say, singular—person will find his way through all of this. If the weight of custom is the challenge to a person starting to be a adult, then custom, one way or another, must be made less of. This is easier said than done. Prufrock poignantly concludes:

We have lingered in the chambers of the sea
By sea-girls wreathed with seaweed red and brown
Till human voices wake us, and we drown. (1936, 17)

Custom is defeated in the chambers of the sea, but we can only linger, not live, there. The undersea world is, literally and symbolically, the world of the dream. In it, as we have seen, the dream ego has the openness of the child. The sea-girls are seductive, forthcoming, attentive. But when we are awakened into the reality of our ordinary, "real" lives, we drown. The magical, metaphor-driven world of the dream is cancelled out by the ordinariness of those human voices we now know too well, talking of Michelangelo, or declaring "That is not it, at all." No wonder Prufrock drowns in them. So may we, in early adulthood.

Those human voices represent the impersonal, detached, anonymous collective: what we call "society," or "the real world." It is a world that may be welcomed by, say, "well-adjusted" extroverts; or it may be feared and avoided, as it is by some introverts. In its fiercest form, this fear and avoidance drives some people to the creation of a separate reality. The most dramatic instance of this is the schizophrenic's creation of an idiosyncratic, fantastic (that is, fantasy-located) unique world. But even without psychosis the terrors may come upon us, as we know from nightmares. In them we enter a terrifying world, populated by those images that derive from the shadow side of our existence. The magic lantern can throw *our* nerves in patterns on a screen, as Prufrock imagined it could. Wordsworth, too, knew this experience. In *The Prelude*, he wrote of "a huge peak, black and huge" that loomed over him. Then, it "with a purpose of its own / And measured motion like a living thing, / Strode after me ...." And afterward,

... o'er my thoughts
There hung a darkness, call it solitude
Or blank desertion. No familiar shapes
Remained, no pleasant images of trees,
Of sea or sky, no colors of green fields;

> But huge and mighty forms, that do not live
> Like living men, moved slowly through the mind,
> By day, and were a trouble to my dreams ...

(1948, 243–244)

The crucial difference between Wordsworth and Eliot's Prufrock is that Wordsworth has his entire experience *alone*. Prufrock, in early adulthood, cannot be alone. He must remain aware of those women and his secret, frightened self. He is caught between his true self and a persona of impersonality that the women require. Prufrock wants desperately to be seen, but at the same time he is terrified that it is the chaos within him that will become visible. It is not that the women will see him, but that they will see *through* him. Even if his nerves are thrown in patterns on a screen, he will not matter. If the archetypes have the power to confer order, they also have the power to embody chaos. The sleeping giant of Hall's childhood was also a "huge and mighty form." Confronted with such, a child feels, at first, powerless; and this may lead to a feeling that never entirely vanishes. Prufrock, because he is unseen by those around him, lives with the primal ("overwhelming") question: What it would be like not to exist at all?

Not to exist at all. We enter here the fearsome aspect of the archetypal ground. If the archetypes have the power to confer order, they also have the power to embody chaos. Consider again the idea, advanced in Chapter One, that the archetypes "wait," so to speak, for a particular person to pick up his or her unique configuration of them—that configuration being determined by a combination of innate potentials in the individual which then combine with particular events in the world. In my own case, the mother archetype was tied to death and an afterlife, right from the start. We do not know Prufrock's history, but we can make some plausible guesses. The archetype of the hero, the doer, came up against some experience that made action seem impossible to him, or at least full of risk. He approaches action ("Let us go...") but then does not act.

Perhaps the person within Prufrock who cannot act is entirely fearful. If this is the case—and we cannot know—then that scared person always holds back, does not "go," does not ask the overwhelming question even though he knows what it is. On our hero/victim scale, Prufrock envisions himself a victim, in spite of his carefully constructed persona. On our order/chaos schema, his outer life is superficially orderly—too much so—but his inner life, the one he is trying to show us, is full of contradictions and psychic wounds. All this prevents him from acting effectively in the world. (This has been said of Hamlet. But there is, I am convinced, a crucial difference between Hamlet and Prufrock: Hamlet can and does act in the outer world. He arranges for the play within the play. He confronts his mother. He arranges the deaths of Rosencrantz and Guildenstern—and so on. Prufrock cannot act. Nevertheless, it is no accident that Prufrock pictures himself as a minor character in Hamlet. Prufrock can imagine himself playing a part, rather than being a person. But, I say again, Prufrock's problem is that he cannot go out into the world and be effective in it, even in ordinary ways. His inability to act has an archetypal foundation. The pain and helplessness of Prufrock has been brought on by the presence of forces larger than he is, forces which threaten to overwhelm ("drown") him. Here we approach the condition of schizophrenia, where the archetypal dominates the ego.

In Jungian terms, he is in the grip of a *complex*. The complex is a part of Prufrock that acts as a separate character within him, a character in conflict with his own, conscious best interests. Prufrock's obvious task is to make his way in the world. The complex is afraid to do this, and this is why the conflict between the complex and the conscious person arises. Prufrock fears that women will not listen to him; the complex may have its origin there. We cannot know, but it is a plausible guess.

One theoretical note about complexes: we have seen that the complex is in conflict with the whole person. It is important to note that the complex itself is always partial, always one-sided, and therefore always in conflict with wholeness. The archetype of wholeness is what Jung called the Self, with a capital S. The Self includes everything, and is by definition in balance: it is ordered perfectly, but therefore very hard to apprehend. It may be represented, though: the Egyptian feather-image of Maat is one such representation; gold, as the purest substance, is another. Jung made much of the mandala as a Self symbol, because mandalas are structured as wheels containing opposed elements arranged with precise symmetry. The rose that Dante and Beatrice see at the end of the *Paradiso* is mandala-like and symbolizes the perfection of God. Herakles' vision reflected in his cry, "*Splendour! It All Coheres!*" is an expression of his intuition of the Self as an entity, and of its wholeness; he has been hero and is now victim. We will amplify this concept when we come to the Old Age chapter. For poor Prufrock, such a structure is almost unimaginable, but he does have slight intimations of it. The mermaids, because they contain opposites, fish and human, are a hint of it. But Prufrock's life is too dominated by the scared-person complex to allow him the peace and order that may come with age. Wordsworth was far more fortunate. He could, and did, write of "truths that wake, / To perish never..." Imperishable truths are not part of Prufrock's world. It may be argued, and it has been, that Prufrock is Eliot, and Eliot's childhood and upbringing have been cited as being reflected in Prufrock, but this just takes us afield and raises the whole thorny and distracting issue of the artist in relation to his art. Rather than pursuing that tangent, I return to my own experience, where I can be surer of identifying complexes when they manifested themselves, for good or ill, unseen as they were when they came upon me.

Here, then, are two pieces of my own history from this time in my life. I write of two women, both carriers of complexes within me. One seemed (and was!) miraculously wonderful when we met, and she has remained a close and loyal friend for fifty years. For me, the wonder—or is it enchantment?—endures. The other, whom I met five years later, became my first wife. We met by chance, but we shared a history we didn't know about until after we were very much in love.

We had two children together, and they have grown into exemplary adults, I am happy to say. But I begin with the earlier experience, my meeting up with S., and something of our years since.

I have mentioned my first coming upon *The Love Song of J. Alfred Prufrock*, and my surprise when I suddenly recognized that I had had an inner life all along, and how that discovery caused me to switch my major from zoology to English. The change, not made until the end of my sophomore year, meant I had fallen behind academically, and would have to take a summer course in my new major in order to graduate with my class. So, on the second of July, 1954, I found myself in the entryway of St. Hilda's College, Oxford, where we

"S," 1954

extramural students were to live for the first half of the summer session. Two Yale classmates would be there, too, but I hadn't seen them, either in London or arriving in Oxford. There was a bulletin board next to the Junior Common Room with notices on it meant for us new arrivals. As I went up to read what was there, I saw an ethereally beautiful young woman, gamine-like, in a much-traveled raincoat. She looked as if she had always been at Oxford, as if she were part of a world I had not yet entered and knew nothing about. But she was reading the bulletin board herself. I felt an overwhelming and therefore scary hope that she was actually another arriving student. We spoke. She was. Her voice was as soft and unfamiliar as everything else about her. We made a date for a drink at a local pub after dinner.

The pub was dark and smoky and people were playing darts and shove ha'penny. We found a tiny table and I asked S. what she wanted. "Grand Marnier," she said. I had no idea what that was, but it sounded French. At the bar, my imitation of S. saying Grand Marnier was, to my relief, just good enough: the barkeeper produced a little glass of a golden liqueur. I forget what I had; probably a beer. But S. gave me a taste of her liqueur, and I found it extraordinary: alcohol together with pure sweet orange. My education had begun. And that afternoon we had found out, to my unspeakable (and unspoken) delight, that we were to be together in a tutorial. Its topic was modern poetry, and it was to be taught by John Bayley.

John Bayley had just finished his M.A. at Oxford. His tutorial met in a nondescript classroom in venerable New College. I think there were about eight of us altogether. We were John's first teaching assignment at Oxford. He was a bit nervous just because of that, and because most of us were Americans. When John began to speak, I was startled and then overwhelmed with anxiety: he had a severe speech impediment. He would stop, sometimes in the middle of a word. Just *stop*. He did not even breathe. I found the silence agonizing. I had barely begun to think of myself as wanting to become a teacher, and my identification with any other teacher was therefore immediate and profound. I was anguished and felt John must be too. But, after a dreadful moment, he would resume as if nothing had happened. I looked over at S. She was calm, interested, attending to the discussion. That helped me calm down. After a few meetings of the tutorial we both noticed that John, far from being troubled by his blocked speech, was *using* those pauses. He was thinking within them, searching for the exact next word. Over and over again he found it. It was as if he planted the poems in us and then, in his words and his silences, their meanings grew on their own. He is one of the most magical teachers I have ever had. That summer he was also courting—eventually successfully—Iris Murdoch. In later years he went on to become Warton Professor of English Literature at Oxford. It was a wonder and a privilege to know him at the very beginning of his great life in scholarship, teaching, and criticism. (In 1998 I saw John again, at a conference outside of London, and was able to thank him at last. How seldom do we have a chance to thank our teachers!)

S. and I developed something of a routine. We would keep talking about the poems we'd discussed and, because it was almost always cold and foggy, we would then go back to her room for sherry. The sherry and the company were as comforting as S.'s gas fireplace, into which we sometimes had to put a shilling for warmth. Once, though, the day was warm and even sunny, so we sat by the river Cherwell instead—a rare treat. Bayley's class had been about a poem by either Auden or Hopkins. Whatever poem it was, I didn't agree with John's reading of it, and I began saying so to S. The more I talked, and the more she listened, the more I became carried away. How could he possibly say *that?* It has to be *this!* And so on. Then, all at once, I was startled to feel S.'s fingers just grazing the back of my hand. Her touch silenced me instantly, and she looked straight at me. Softly she said, "Don't be so upset." In that moment, the whole world around me returned: there was the river, and rough green grass, and the cooing of doves, and S's hand, with a bracelet made of a single gold wire around her wrist, still touching mine.

After all these years, I have never forgotten that moment. S.'s concern was entirely for my well-being, which is to say, my peace of mind, in the profound sense of that phrase. I had been truly seen and cared for. My parents, faced with their son carrying on so loudly, would have felt *their* discomfort, *their* embarrassment in the presence of such noisy arguing, but I doubt that they would have said or done anything. S.'s concern, instead, was entirely for me. She knew that I had violated all three of the Greek maxims: know thyself, moderation in all things, honor the gods. I had lost track of myself, and she brought me back. Moderation was gone, but S.'s gentle touch restored it. I had lost sight of the gods: I had put my own construction of things above everything else. I was truly "upset," in the metaphoric sense of that word. S. saw all this, and gave me back myself. She has been doing this for me (in real life and in my imagining) ever since. I still use the memory of that touch to quiet myself, to center myself, in the midst of inner or outer disorder.

Gerard Manley Hopkins' poem *Duns Scotus' Oxford* still captures, for me, the place and its peace:

Towery city and branchy between towers,
Cuckoo-echoing, bell-swarmed, lark-charmed, rook-racked,
    river-rounded,
The dapple-eared lily below thee... (1966, 58)

But everything comes to an end. My parents came to pick me up in a little Austin A-40 that we would use to tour around Germany, France and Austria—their version of a grand tour for me. (The car was to become mine for my senior year.) They met S., briefly, and I imagine they could see immediately why I was ambivalent about leaving with them. But off we went. And there were memorable moments: sleeping in a bathtub in Ulm; *Don Giovanni* in Salzburg; my twenty-first birthday dinner at a three-star restaurant in the Burgundy country. The sommelier insisted that I must have wine from the year of my birth: alas, I'm one year too old for 1934, which was a great vintage. Nevertheless, the wine tasted fine to me. S., of course, *was* born in 1934.

I returned to Yale in the fall, and I, in my little black car with its red leather seats, found my way to S. and her college, Smith, right away. We saw each other often. We ate well in a country inn, sat in the dark in my little car, and talked—or didn't. Once, S. had to write a paper about Walt Whitman. Neither of us knew a thing about him. We spent a day in an empty classroom, reading poems to one another and writing our thoughts on the blackboard until it was full of notes and ideas and an emerging structure for a paper. We had joined together in the kind of high dialogue that results—with luck—in understanding, in seeing deeply into the poems, and much more. S. came to Yale, too: I have snapshots of her, reading, in my room; and we went to at least one meeting of a subtle and profound seminar on the European Epic. S. went with me to Old Black Point, and she once went, with my parents, to watch me playing cricket for Yale. I'd learned the game at Oxford, obviously, and I can't imagine a greater test of patience than to watch such a slow and incomprehensible game. But she did; and she came to New York, too, and met my grandmother.

S. and her mother lived in Cambridge, Massachusetts, and I visited there, too. Her mother was an important editor for a major publisher; she specialized in fiction. She welcomed me, but not in any usual superficially polite way. Rather, she took me in as a person who was interested in reading, in books, in what happens inside people as they turn pages. Whenever I came, it seemed there were famous writers and editors and Harvard professors, over for tea or drinks. It was a world I had no knowledge of, but I was an eager and interested person, and I was at Yale, which made me slightly unusual in Cambridge circles. S.'s mother encouraged my questions, she told me about editing, she listened, she was patient. I began to understand where her daughter had learned those things. I never felt cast into the role of the youthful outsider. S.'s mother was one of the great, gracious people I have ever known. I can still see, in my mind's eye, her living room, and I can hear the voices there. There was gentle but intense excitement, always.

S. and I have remained the best of friends, as I have said, for more than fifty years now. (She would never say to me what Prufrock feared, always, to hear: "That is not it, at all." She would, instead, ask again, gently, and wait for me to become settled, or clearer.) We had, I now see, something together that was (and is) in some ways better than being in love. I have said what S. gave me; I believe I have always been, for her, a person who has cared, and paid attention, but who was not caught by the unconscious webs that "love" spins in early adulthood. Because of her great beauty, I am sure—I know, in fact—that many men saw her as someone put on earth to meet their narcissistic needs, rather than seeing her as who she is. Beauty can be a terrible problem.

S.'s quiet, constant kindness was a new experience for me. She thereby became, I later learned, an "anima figure" for me. I see from my dreams of her that this is so, but the anima is also largely an aspect of my life that remains on the "bottom" line of the transference diagram (below). The importance of the anima is that it is the equivalent, in the unconscious, of the persona. That is to say, the anima acts as a bridge between conscious awareness and unconscious domains. Thus S., as anima figure, educated me, and still does. I mean "educate" in its root meaning: "to lead out of." This is the anima as guide. I met S. at the exact moment when a guide was necessary, when I had taken my first step toward my life's work and my first step into what I thought was adulthood. As I took that step, there she was. (That is how the world is supposed to work!) I sometimes still feel, when I am with S., the way I did when we first met: the ordinary world recedes into the middle distance, and we are, instead, together in a place the two of us have made up.

Step back now and look at relationship and its archetypal underpinnings. I will set out a theory of relationships—what they are and how they develop—and then apply it in this chapter to myself and S., and to my first marriage. In the following chapter I take up my second (and continuing!) marriage—as an example of a more conscious connection between two people.

The beginning of any important relationship is almost entirely within the unconscious minds of the two people involved. In a seminal essay, "The Psychology of the Transference," Jung laid out a model for the structure of a relationship, and I depend on that model here. Jung's ostensible topic is the transference, a technical term for the relationship with the psychoanalyst that develops within the patient as she or he undergoes analysis. But Jung's description is applicable to all relationships. Here, with his specialized terms dropped, is the generalized situation of two people who have some connection—good or bad—between them:

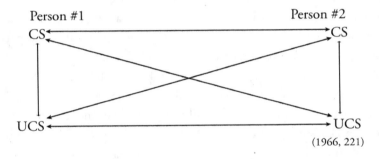

(1966, 221)

The relationship at the conscious level (top line) is what each person sees and knows about the other. It is a relationship between two egos; everything is "aboveboard." More precisely, at the very beginning of the relationship, the conscious connection is between two personas, given that the persona is what we present to the outside world. Prufrock presents himself as conservatively dressed, conventional, meticulous. The women no doubt see him this way, with the result that the conscious relationship is conventional, too. But, as this is going on, each person is also connected to his or her own unconscious. Prufrock imagines what it would be like if his unconscious constructions were to become public: it is "as if a magic lantern threw the nerves in patterns on a screen." But he never lets this show. His relationships, even with the reader, his newly found companion, remain one-sided. It is no wonder he is lonely.

When S. and I met, I had been taking care of myself by myself for a very long time. There were, inside me, a person who needed care, and a person who was the caregiver. Early on, I began to feel cared for by S. Not that she was in any way trying to fulfill this role; it was just how she was. Why did I feel this so soon? Because I had projected that caregiver part of myself (which was of course unconscious) onto S. In the diagram above, such a projection would be indicated by an arrow proceeding diagonally up from my unconscious to S.'s conscious person. Now, it is true that she had to have some element of the caregiver within her in order for my projection to "take." But when I was with her, especially at the beginning, I was experiencing a part of myself. And I am sure I was—am—a part of her, too, but because of her intriguing demureness I am not quite sure what part. A person more free to pursue ideas, perhaps? S. was a brilliant student of, among other things, classical Greek, but she did leave college to marry, while I stayed in college and then went on to graduate schools. So I may represent, to her, an unlived part of her life. S. and I did not, in the way I will define it, "fall in love," because what we projected into one another was so precisely delineated. Wonderful and comforting, yes, but not "everything." This closeness has been, and is, miracle enough for me.

Projection originates all relationships. Because it is an unconscious process, it is never perceived for what it is. But it is real nevertheless. For example, if a man says (traditionally, to a bartender), "My wife doesn't understand me," the chances are good that there is a part of him that doesn't understand his wife. But it isn't macho to admit to not understanding women, so this man projects his own non-understanding person onto his wife. Now he sees her as "owning" what he has projected onto her, and this is how he reports the situation. "My wife doesn't understand me" is, from the man's point of view, entirely true. There is indeed a person who doesn't understand. It is a part of the man, but it is an unconscious part, too shameful to own up to consciously. There does have to be a bit of the wife that really doesn't understand something of her husband. This is the "hook" that catches the projection, making "my wife doesn't understand me" feel completely objective and valid to the speaker. Prufrock gives us another example of this dynamic. He imagines that the woman to whom he will try to tell a profound truth ("I am Lazarus, come from the dead, come back to tell you all ...") will simply ignore him, will disdainfully tell him, "That is not what I meant at all. That is not it, at all." What part of Prufrock is "not interested"? *Not to be interested in the world is a way of defending one-self against what the world may hold.* So Prufrock projects this aspect of himself onto the women around him, and thus drives himself further into isolation. Remember, though, that there is a part of these women that is genuinely not interested—the part that is reserved and withholding, as their social class dictates. That is the hook. But Prufrock is the one who is caught in the depressing loneliness caused by how he sees his world. The scared child, or the victim, needs care and attention, but neither Prufrock nor the women can give these things with any ease or understanding. I needed care and attention, too. S. provided them, and still does.

So far we have looked at the top line of our diagram, the conscious relationship, and at the diagonal lines, which represent projections from one person onto the other, those projections then being seen as factually true aspects of the other. The bottom line represents the totally unconscious relationship—unconscious, obviously, on both sides. Inchoate feelings may be generated there, but its very unconsciousness makes this dimension inaccessible. So it is those diagonal lines that command our attention. I turn now to a brief description of my own first marriage, in order to, among other things, look more closely at the phenomenon called "falling in love."

Amy Hoyt and I met in graduate school; we were in a program offered by the Harvard Graduate School of Education designed to prepare liberal arts graduates for careers as secondary school teachers. I had done a year of graduate work toward a Ph.D. in English after

Yale, but then a time in the army as a company clerk gave me a compelling interest in problems of basic literacy. I decided to teach young people, and so, in 1958, found myself at Harvard. In a philosophy of education class there was, in the back row, a young woman, to whom I said, "You have to get here early to get a seat." We survived my staggering lack of originality. She was blonde, and from California, with that state's outdoor freshness about her, and she had an air of confidence. We liked each other right away. If S. was a caregiver, my wife-to-be was (I felt) a different, much more familiar, sort. I had (I thought) become more adult, more "independent," and I projected this onto her, too. Amy and I were constructing our professional selves, as teachers. So had my mother, when she decided to become an artist. Amy and my mother were alike in how they walked, talked, and thought. Of course I didn't see this so clearly at first. But we had been brought up in similar worlds, and we recognized this increasingly as we came to know one another. It wasn't long before we had decided to marry.

This is one form of "falling in love." It is the mutual discovery of feeling just like the other. "I feel as if I've known you all my life," lovers declare at the beginning of their relationship. It is true. They have known all the parts of themselves that they have projected onto the other. In the case of "falling in love," there are many such parts, enough to make up perhaps almost all of each person's psyche. If S. and I had, and have, one deep thing, Amy and I had a huge, shared store of values and experiences. More importantly, we had an assured sense of who we were for one another, because we were the same as our parents. Thus we were completely at ease from the start, and this, I think, is one model of what "falling in love" means. It is not, as we shall see, sufficient.

I took Amy down to New York City to meet my parents, and my mother's mother, in whose apartment she was to stay. (At the time, my parents had an apartment literally across the street, where I stayed.) I still remember our getting off the elevator and my grandmother opening the door. I introduced her to Amy Hoyt. "Are you

Andy Hoyt's daughter?" asked my grandmother, still standing in the little entryway of her apartment. Amy was. "Did you know that my husband was Dr. Jim Miller?" No... and, in the entryway, my grandmother told us this story:

Anson ("Andy") Hoyt graduated from Yale and Yale Medical School and trained in pulmonary medicine with Dr. Elliott Trudeau at his tuberculosis sanatorium on Saranac Lake in the Adirondacks in upstate New York. My grandfather had trained there, too. Amy's mother came down with tuberculosis and became a patient of my grandfather's. She spent time at Saranac, and recovered. Then she met Andy Hoyt, and they fell in love, and planned marriage. But first she consulted my grandfather for his opinion of her condition. Could she—should she—marry? Who are you going to marry, asked my grandfather. Andy Hoyt. Oh, said my grandfather, I know Andy— he trained at Saranac. Of course you can marry *him*! So she did, and they moved to California, for the climate. Because of her TB history, they did not have children of their own; they adopted a girl and a boy. But then my wife's mother stayed free of disease for several years, so she went back to my grandfather to ask whether she could bear a child. He gave his approval; she did; and the child was Amy, now standing in my grandmother's doorway while we heard this remarkable narrative. We had had no idea.

Obviously we were closer than we knew. It all felt right somehow. We married, had two children, and led a nomadic academic life. Amy soldiered on, living in what were, for us, some pretty out-of-the-way places: Urbana, Illinois, for example, and Tallahassee, Florida; but also New Haven, and Hanover, New Hampshire, which felt more familiar. We were both bound up in form and ritual. Amy brought traditions from her family: for example, every Christmas, Christmas cookies had to be baked and sent to many relatives. Year after year she made them; our children eventually joined in, sprinkling red and blue and yellow sugar on each one. Birthday parties for the children had a ritual feel to them, too: there were many games, wonderfully organized by Amy, who turned into an exemplary "cruise director" for such activities—a role I could not even imagine myself taking on. There is a photograph I made of the two of us, celebrating Christmas Eve in our first home, a tiny, almost windowless basement apartment in Urbana. We are sitting across from one another at our little dining room table. We are all dressed up, Amy in a dark blue party dress. On the table a bottle of wine resides on a silver wine coaster, and there is a large silver candelabra, as there would have been in our parents' homes. We are contented and smiling.

In "The Psychology of the Transference," Jung wrote:

> This bond [the "transference neurosis"] is often of such intensity that we could almost speak of a "combination." When two chemical substances combine, both are altered. This is precisely what happens in the transference. (171)

This mutual altering is a sign of a good, ongoing relationship. But Amy and I were already so similar that it felt as if there was nothing to alter on either side. In such a relationship, *nothing happens*. When there is no grain of sand in the oyster, no pearl is formed. This was not noticeable when we were young, and raising children, and making our way. Besides, we had the bond of my grandfather's role in Amy's very existence. Looking back at it, of course, it seems a little like a Sophoclean play, with fate controlling events. Youth cancels out such reflection; we were comfortably together.

"Nothing happens" is an indictment of a marriage. But I was working too hard to notice. In 1969–1970, I was finishing my Ph.D. dissertation and teaching at Yale. In September we had bought a small house and were living in Hamden, Connecticut, where our children had started school (we could all see The Sleeping Giant from our upstairs windows). Then, in October, we found out (from a neighbor, not from any administrator, or from the person who had hired me) that the program I was teaching in was going to be terminated in June, and I would be out of a job. We were obviously angry, and scared. Academic jobs were scarce, and I began a search immediately, but with no results. At the same time Amy, who had long suffered from debilitating vertigo, saw an advertisement asking for volunteers to be treated for that condition as part of an experiment being done by Yale's psychology department. She signed up; it was a program based on behavior modification. She was treated by a very prepossessing older man who was making a career change. A powerful idealizing transference developed in Amy, and he had no training in the handling of it. Amy began drinking, secretly.

Neither the children nor I were aware of this. In May of 1970 Yale was the scene of massive anti–Vietnam War protests. National Guardsmen patrolled the streets; tear gas was in the air everywhere. I stayed downtown, teaching, but also photographing and working with local media. Amy was frightened; I was exhilarated. By May I had secured a new position. We made the move to New Hampshire and bought a house there, but were then unable to sell the one in Hamden; we had two mortgage payments, and it was a difficult time. Not until the following summer, when we were staying with my parents at Old Black Point, did my mother tell me she thought Amy had a drinking problem. I denied it; I hadn't seen it. It was true, though. Two years later we moved again: I had a new faculty position, this time with tenure and a doubled salary, and I thought the new security would solve everything. Of course it didn't, but my thinking was characteristic of early adulthood: the idea that solutions to inner problems are to be found in the outside world.

Because we were so similar in our ways and customs and upbringing, Amy and I had, as I've said, an unexamined marriage. In effect, we were reenacting the sort of relationship we thought adults like us—our parents, in other words—had. I believe, now, that the man Amy saw for her vertigo in New Haven provided an experience—without meaning to—of the possibility of a different kind of relationship. Not necessarily better; just different. Not that he did or even said anything unethical. I imagine this as the sort of thing that gets transmitted along the bottom, unconscious line in the transference diagram. But when one has retreated, as we had done, so completely into a world of familiar form, critical introspection about anything is hard to do. In our world of form, introspection was something that "just isn't done," as Prufrock so painfully knew. Looking inside is looking down, toward the unconscious. Looking down is also the source of fear in vertigo. Alcohol dissolves fear. Besides this, Amy had to contend with me, a husband whose focus was far too much on work, on getting ahead; I traveled to conventions and gave papers and did workshops and was preoccupied.

However, I began to do more of the household chores because Amy was often asleep by the time I got home; the children now knew about the drinking and what it was doing to their mother, and even worked out a code they could use to telephone me at my office to alert me to bring home food for dinner, or whatever. I was furious, frustrated and exhausted. I saw other women, and was by turns consumed with excitement and guilt. Four years into all this, I told Amy that unless she joined AA I would seek a divorce, but this made no difference; she never went to a meeting. We were divorced in 1977. Two years later, Amy was hospitalized with alcoholic cirrhosis, her belly grossly swollen with ascites. Her condition deteriorated. During my last visit with her, she denied that she ever had a drinking problem, and spoke of planning to make Christmas cookies after her discharge, because she had always done so for us and for our families. She died two days later.

There is another part of Amy's history connected to her alcoholism. She was the natural child of her parents, but her older brother and sister were adopted. Amy's parents treated Amy as the special one: she was sent to better schools and an excellent college, and she had her junior year in Switzerland—and so on. It is a huge burden to be thus privileged. Amy felt, I think, profoundly guilty, and she also felt she had to be a paragon. It is no wonder that problems that would not trouble most people loomed large in her mind. For example, her mother became ill with TB again when Amy was five years old, and was sent to a sanatorium, this time for two years. Dr. Hoyt continued his research and was distant, so there was a succession of caretakers, maids, and nannies (another experience Amy and I shared). A small child, especially the "favored" one, can develop an exaggerated feeling of having power—*even the power of being able to make mother sick*. But in Amy's case the Oedipal fantasy of having father to herself never really came true. Dr. Hoyt was charming: he occasionally brought home from his lab a live mouse dyed blue or red. But more often he was very distant, and very busy.

So there was within Amy a deep hole, so to speak, an unfilled place where there should have been an assured, confident person. Instead there was a guilty, and therefore, unconsciously, an undeserving one. Thus anything that happened—like our meeting up, for example—had this cloud hanging over it. An unconscious cloud, to be sure, but absolutely real. This puts the story of my grandfather giving Amy's mother permission to marry, and then to have a child, in another light. It makes Amy's very existence a strange, overly fortuitous circumstance. I have tried to intuit how this affected her, and us. For me, there is no doubt I was repeating a pattern lived out by my parents within a marriage made possible by my mother's father, but with no conscious awareness of doing so. For Amy, there was that undeserving person I have mentioned. Her life had depended upon two permissions from my grandfather, a doctor outside her family, but within mine. Looking at all this in more general terms, early adulthood consists of (1) establishing a plausible persona; (2) making one's way in the world; and (3) unconsciously following patterns already laid down by one's parents, or other close elders. All three go on at the same time. This amounts to being pulled in several directions at once. Which "direction" will dominate at any given moment depends on the outer circumstances and the arrangement of complexes that are pertinent. All of it can be troubling. The outer and the inner world compete, and may be in profound conflict. The hero/victim, chaos/order polarities can seem all-encompassing.

Their strength derives, in part, from a singular feature of early adulthood. In contrast to every other stage of life described in this work, early adulthood is not shaped by a direct connection to the archetypal ground. It is too consumed by persona, imitation, and superficial worldliness. The task of becoming an individual—the heroic quest, in other words—is subordinated to pressing, but outer, concerns. It is not surprising that, in our time, the most coveted "demographic" for television advertisers is the cohort of people in this stage of life. It is in the interest of advertisers to encourage people to confuse individuation with the ownership, or use of, particular products or services. Coca-Cola used to be "the pause that refreshes," an idea that applies to a person of any age. But a competing product later addressed itself to "the Pepsi Generation," a very specific appeal to one group of people. Unfortunately, the media's pressure to use disposable income as an expression of individuality through product choice can render real individuality almost unachievable. As Wordsworth, in a famous sonnet, lamented,

> The world is too much with us; late and soon,
> Getting and spending, we lay waste our powers:
> Little we see in nature that is ours;
> We have given our hearts away, a sordid boon! (1948, 236)

A dark but appropriate view of this time in our life, and the larger culture as well. Then, as he does in the *Intimations* ode, Wordsworth moves on to describe a way out of this limited way of living:

> Great God! I'd rather be
> A Pagan suckled in a creed outworn;
> So might I, standing on this pleasant lea,
> Have glimpses that would make me less forlorn;
> Have sight of Proteus rising from the sea,... (1948, 236)

Wordsworth, like Prufrock, stands on the shore and imagines myth come to life. In early adulthood we have been inland, on the deceptively solid ground of making something of our life in the world. But the sea is always there. It offered mermaids to J. Alfred Prufrock. He can see them, even if he does not think they will sing to him. And seeing them is a promising sign. It suggests that we, too, can see things beyond ordinary experience, habit and custom, the very custom that can be such a deadening presence in early adulthood. It is this seeing to which we turn in the following chapter, because it will lead us toward true becoming. The archetypal ground, like the sea, is always there. Even if we lose our connection to it for a time, we have within us the possibility of recovering it. As T. S. Eliot wrote:

> Not fare well,
> But fare forward, voyagers. (1943, 26)

CHAPTER 6

TRUE ADULTHOOD
TRUTHS THAT WAKE

The thought of our past years in me doth breed
Perpetual benediction: not indeed
For that which is most worthy to be blest;
Delight and liberty, the simple creed
Of Childhood, whether busy or at rest,
With new-fledged hopes still fluttering in his breast:—
Not for these I raise
The song of thanks and praise...

. . . .

But for those first affections,
Those shadowy recollections,
Which, be they what they may,
Are yet the fountain-light of all our day,
Are yet a master-light of all our seeing;
Uphold us, cherish, and have power to make
Our noisy years seem moments in the being
Of the eternal Silence: truths that wake,
To perish never:
Which neither listlessness, nor mad endeavor,

Nor Man nor Boy,
Nor all that is at enmity with joy,
Can utterly abolish or destroy.
Hence in a season of calm weather
Though inland far we be,
Our souls have sight of that immortal sea
Which brought us hither... (1948, 132–139, 147–163)

W<small>E HAVE UNDERSTOOD</small> early adulthood as a time of preoccupation, rather than occupation; affections, but not "first affections"; a time of paradoxically relevant distractions. Relevant, because getting along in the world is obviously to be desired; distractions, because the meaning of an experience can get lost in its very immediacy. We come now to consider what happens when we give up, or at least let go of for a time, this preoccupation. In 1935, T. S. Eliot suggested, in a letter to Stephen Spender, "You don't really criticize any author to whom you have never surrendered yourself.... Even just the bewildering minute counts; you have to give yourself up, and then recover yourself.... Of course the self recovered is never the same as the self before it was given" (1975, 13). Describing an idealized process by which the artist takes in the world, Eliot wrote, "What happens is a continual surrender of himself as he is at the moment to something which is more valuable" (1950, 6–7). We have in the previous chapter discussed the person "as he is at the moment," caught in ordinary life. We turn now to the surrendering of that person to something larger. The artist is a paradigm for this because the artist, in contrast to most of us, is always engaged in the process of making something new. This by itself undermines custom. Here is a passage by Peter Galassi about the American photographer Walker Evans:

> Thus he [Walker Evans] was free to adopt the clinician's pitiless scrutiny of society, and the whole vocabulary of descriptive photography, in the service of the inexplicable dictates of his flickering intuitions. The prospect excited Evans so much that in 1930 he told his friend Lincoln Kirstein that he sometimes thought he would go mad. The intensity of vision that he sought and repeatedly found had been described (although without the least thought of photography) by his hero Baudelaire: "In certain almost supernatural states of being, the depth of life reveals itself in its entirety in the sight before one's eyes, however ordinary it may be. The latter becomes the symbol of the former." (2000, 16)

"Intensity of vision," indeed. The visions that for Prufrock were immediately undone by *re*visions are now made permanent by art and insight. The constant questioning of insightful perception by the prosaic outside world is now challenged by the exhilaration of the vision itself. But these are the visions of artists. What of more ordinary folk? What of us? This chapter is about the sorts of experiences that can—and do—shake us out of custom, and form, and habit, and so move us along in our lives. The life of *outer* form, that is, life informed by custom or habit, pales, in midlife, but often there seems to be nothing to take its place. This type of the midlife crisis has as its primary symptom a general feeling of "there must be more to life than this." This very statement is often exactly what a person seeking psychoanalysis—especially Jungian analysis—starts with in the initial session. More generally, it is a feeling that often initiates changes of all kinds: travel, divorce, new work. For Baudelaire, there were moments when "the depth of life reveals itself in its entirety." But for most other people, there is no such revelation because there seems to be no depth to life. They have realized that living the "necessary impersonal life" is deeply unsatisfying, and yet there seems to be nothing else.

That impersonal life, as we have seen, is dominated by consciousness, combined with a collection of unexamined, form-driven assumptions about how things have been and should be. Consciousness, with its smug presumption that it knows everything that matters, is always undermined by new experience. Years ago, Willard Waller cited "four wishes" that make up a set of needs that must be satisfied, somehow, for us all:

- The wish for response
- The wish for recognition
- The wish for new experience
- The wish for security. (1933, 135)

Each of these relates to one of the others. "Response" means the fundamental mirroring that must exist between, say, a mother and her infant; but it also means the need we all share to have our immediate situation seen for what it is *to us*. When S. saw my distress about our teacher's idea of the meaning of a poem, she responded to it, and therefore to me. "Recognition" is different: recognition means being rewarded in the public domain for something done there. A child's drawing stuck up on the refrigerator door recognizes an achievement in school. Much of early midlife is a quest for recognition. "New experience" means just what it says, but it can be a problem, because new experience is often in conflict with the fourth wish, "security." Security flows from a predictable world; new experience, by definition, is unpredictable. The tension underlying the loss of meaning in life at this stage is caused by the conflict between seeking new experience and the fear of leaving security behind in doing so. This is the story of a truly great book: the *Odyssey*. Odysseus's goal is to return to Ithaca, to his wife and son, and to restore order to his kingdom. But Odysseus is an inveterate explorer, a seeker after new experience. He *needs* to hear the sirens' song, so he leaves his ears unstoppered and lashes himself to his ship's mast. Tennyson, continuing the story, imagines Odysseus, having returned and living quietly at home, becoming restless. Tired of security, he yearns once again for new experience:

> I am a part of all that I have met;
> Yet all experience is an arch wherethrough
> Gleams that untravelled world, whose margin fades
> Forever and forever when I move.
> How dull it is to pause, to make an end,
> To rust unburnished, not to shine in use,
> As though to breathe were life...
>
> Come, my friends,
> 'Tis not too late to seek a newer world.
> Push off, and setting well in order smite
> The sounding furrows; for my purpose holds
> To sail beyond the sunset, and the baths
> Of all the western stars, until I die. (1968, 843)

It is this tension, I think, that underlies this stage of life. Now, if we take the archetypal ground as a fact, then it follows that "new experience" is always there for the having. Every night, the dream is new to us. And beyond that, the world itself is suggestively fraught with unexpected images, if we could but see. It is here that the ordinary person, the person we are every day, can approach the condition of the artist, who sees "the depth of life." Galassi, quoting Baudelaire: "...the depth of life reveals itself in its entirety in the sight before one's eyes, however ordinary it may be. The latter becomes the symbol of the former." That is, the ordinary becomes the symbol of the depth of life. *The ordinary becomes symbolic.* It is this movement toward the symbolic that can, and does, give meaning to life at this stage.

Look again at the dream presented earlier. A man, in retirement, finds himself embarking on a trip across a river. At his age, the meaning of such an image is obvious enough, and we have, from Egyptian mythology, and from the *Odyssey*, the *Aeneid*, and the *Divine Comedy*, ample evidence of a universal image: the crossing of the river that divides life and death. The dreamer, in his conscious, ordinary life, has no "reason" to contemplate the end of his life. He is in fine health, and there is no person near him who is ill or dying. Yet here is his dream. The dream is an image which is both a fact and beyond consciousness at the same time. This is a paradox. What has happened is that the limits of consciousness have been exposed. Consciousness, naturally, wants nothing to do with crossing the river. Consciousness wants to go to the coffee shop, or to travel to New Orleans, or to converse with friends. Consciousness is action and order and predictability—and pleasure. The dream presents the opposite: darkness, threat, fate.

We have seen, in the previous chapter, the consequences of living as if the outer world is all there is. Not that the inner world is banished; rather, it is condemned as the source of problems and puzzles and, as Prufrock says, it is therefore the source of an overwhelming question. Hamlet feels this way, too. He ponders suicide but cannot answer the question of what happens in the afterlife; that question "must give us pause." It certainly gives *him* pause. For our dreamer, though, the image in his dream gives him a partial answer. To be open to such images means having a way to bring to consciousness the whole other side of our being, all that is the opposite of our ordinary or, as we one-sidedly say, "real" world. The awake man doesn't think about the river and the afterlife at all, but the dream ego goes along on what may be the great journey—and participates without reservation, reflection, or fear. Thus within this man there are two personalities, and they are opposites. These two personalities transact with one another. For most people, such transactions are unconscious. Jung had a name for the ability to be aware of such transactions: he called it, I think somewhat unfortunately, the *transcendent function*. He meant by this that the habit-driven split between consciousness and the unconscious is transcended by the symbol—in this case the river—that, if we pay attention to it, forces us to see both at once—"both" meaning life on this side of the river and the unknown on the other side. The dreamer was in analysis, which is really just a way of paying attention. Asked about the river, he associated it with the Styx.

Here is Jung, in a letter:

> There are many normal cases in which, under certain circumstances, a character opposed to the conscious personality suddenly manifests itself, causing a conflict between the two personalities.

> Take the classic case of the temptation of Christ, for example. We say that the devil tempted him, but we could just as well say that an unconscious desire for power confronted him in the form of the devil. Both sides appear here: the light side and the dark. The devil wants to tempt Jesus to proclaim himself master of the world. Jesus wants not to succumb to the temptation; then, thanks to the function that results from every conflict, a symbol appears: it is the idea of the Kingdom of Heaven, a spiritual kingdom rather than a material one.

Two things are united in this symbol, the spiritual attitude of Christ and the devilish desire for power. Thus the encounter of Christ with the devil is a classic example of the transcendent function. It appears here in the form of an involuntary personal experience. But it can be used as a method, too [when we seek the contrary will of the unconscious and confront it in dreams and other unconscious products. In this way the "personality" of the unconscious is brought face-to-face with the counter position of the conscious one]. The resulting conflict—thanks precisely to the transcendent function—leads to a symbol uniting the opposed positions. The symbol cannot be consciously chosen or constructed; it is a sort of intuition or revelation. (1970, 267–268)

The dream, produced as it is at the threshold between conscious and unconscious, is the natural habitat of these spontaneously produced symbols. Hamlet was right to ponder the life/death transition ("To die, to sleep; to sleep, perchance to dream...") in this way. What symbols will be produced, not by us, but *for* us, in our dreams? And produced by what agency?

The problem we all face is that consciousness is limited—very limited. It can give comfortable attention only to what it already knows. A new experience is always at least a challenge and at most an impossibility which will be rejected out of hand. Most dreams are seen this way when we first wake up from them, and some discipline is needed to record them in a timely manner. Consciousness—that is, ego—doesn't like to be derailed. It knows its ways and wants to stick to them. The fact is, though, "There are more things in heaven and earth, Horatio, than are dreamt of in your philosophy," where "philosophy" means science, rationally constructed knowledge, the only sort of knowledge ego is comfortable with. The most awesome knowledge beyond ego is the knowledge of the world of the archetypes, because this world contains images for everything. The sum of all the archetypes is the Self, the "domain" that by definition contains all the pairs of opposites. We have seen it represented by the Egyptian Maat. It is represented also by the Star of David and the Christian cross, where each point, or arm, has its opposite; and by mandala images. Lost souls feel chaos in their waking lives but dream (ideally, at least) of mandalas. The mandala, as Self symbol, is the opposite of chaos, because each aspect within it is balanced by its opposite. The mandala expresses the natural order that is opposed to the daily mess. Jung said any experience of the Self is a defeat for the ego. If the first half of adulthood is ego-dominated, the phase we now consider involves the ego's experience of "something more," something deeper, more complete. The fancy term for this is the *relativization* of the ego. To understand this concept, we must bear in mind Waller's third wish, the wish for new experience, and we must be aware of how such surprise, such unexpectedness, often conflicts with the wish for security. Imagine, then, the person we have described in the previous chapter, but now having vague but persistent feelings of dissatisfaction, even mild depression—dysthymia, as it is called. The salt has lost its savor.

We have already seen that psyche keeps right on producing contrarian symbols no matter what the outer life feels like. This capacity to make symbols may not sound like much of a solution. For the ego alone, it wouldn't be. It is that relativization of the ego, a process urged upon us by the strangeness or unexpectedness of these symbols, to which we must attend.

Creative people—artists, poets, writers—stay open to the symbolic in spite of all sorts of chaos in their lives. Think of Picasso or Jackson Pollock or Andy Warhol, or William Faulkner or Robert Frost, or Tennessee Williams; where the works kept being made despite the ending and beginning of relationships, alcoholism, or drug abuse. Such creative people (one might say, the fortunate ones) stay open to their inner resources no matter what. The rest of us can therefore learn from them. I begin with two passages from the literary criticism of T. S. Eliot. In "Tradition and the Individual Talent," he describes the openness that must be a characteristic of the creating mind.

What happens [in the poet] is a continual surrender of himself as he is at the moment to something which is more valuable. The progress of an artist is a continual self-sacrifice, a continual extinction of personality.

There remains to define this process of depersonalization and its relation to the sense of tradition. It is in this depersonalization that art may be said to approach the condition of science. I, therefore, invite you to consider, as a suggestive analogy, the action which takes place when a bit of finely filiated platinum is introduced into a chamber containing oxygen and sulphur dioxide.

At this point, the first part of Eliot's essay ended; readers of *The Criterion* had to wait for the next issue.

> ... I hinted, by an analogy, that the mind of the mature poet differs from that of the immature one not precisely in any valuation of "personality," not being necessarily more interesting, or having "more to say," but rather by being a more finely perfected medium in which special, or very varied, feelings are at liberty to enter into new combinations.
>
> The analogy was that of the catalyst. When the two gases previously mentioned are mixed in the presence of a filament of platinum, they form sulphurous acid. This combination takes place only if the platinum is present; nevertheless the newly formed acid contains no trace of platinum, and the platinum itself is apparently unaffected; has remained inert, neutral and unchanged. The mind of the poet is the shred of platinum. It may partly or exclusively operate upon the experience of the man himself; but, the more perfect the artist, the more completely separate in him will be the man who suffers and the mind which creates; the more perfectly will the mind digest and transmute the passions which are its material. (1950, 7–8)

"A continual extinction of personality" sounds at first like a radical prescription. But is this not exactly what happens when we experience greatness: our first view of the pyramids, or our first encountering the Marx Brothers? We are in awe, or we are laughing so hard we miss the next wisecrack. This is temporary extinction of personality. Put in the terms we are using here, it is letting go of all ordinariness, all habit, all the details that keep us mired in our ego-driven daily life. The experience Eliot prescribes for the poet is one we can all have, if obviously less often and with less intensity.

Consider the Great Pyramid. It is easy enough to feel the relativization of our ego in the presence of 2,300,000 blocks of stone each *one* weighing, on average, two and a half tons (Lehner, 1997, 108). Or recall being in the presence of comic genius. Here, a famous bit from *Cocoanuts:*

> **Groucho**: [pointing at a map]: All along the river, those are all levees.
> **Chico**: Thatsa the jewish neighborhood.
> **Groucho**: Well, we'll pass over that. Now, here's a little peninsula, and here is a viaduct leading over to the mainland.
> **Chico**: Why a duck?... Why a duck? Why-a-no-chicken?
> **Groucho**: I don't know why-a-no-chicken. I'm a stranger here myself. All I know it's a viaduct. You try to cross over here a chicken, and you'll find out why a duck ....
> (Anobile, 1971, 40–41)

The pyramids and the Marx Brothers are far from ordinary, and we are appropriately lost in admiration. But the real challenge is to be "lost," at least sometimes, in the presence of ordinary daily occurrences, those little things that make up the texture of life. Once again, Eliot, in the process of writing about art, gives us a clue. This passage is from his essay "Hamlet and His Problems." In it, Eliot argues that the play fails because "Shakespeare tackled a problem which proved too much for him (1950)." (Eliot also says "The Hamlet of Laforgue is an adolescent; the Hamlet of Shakespeare is not, he has not that explanation and excuse." As I have indicated, I believe Hamlet can be understood as having that excuse, but I concede I made him adolescent in order to serve my own purposes.)

Here is Eliot's general point, which is extremely useful in the present context:

> The only way of expressing emotion in the form of art is by find-ing an "objective correlative"; in other words, a set of objects, a situation, a chain of events which shall be the formula of that *particular* emotion; such that when the external facts, which must terminate in sensory experience, are given, the emotion is immediately evoked. If you examine any of Shakespeare's more successful tragedies, you will find this exact equivalence; you will find that the state of mind of Lady Macbeth walk-ing in her sleep has been communicated to you by a skillful accumulation of imagined sensory impressions; the words of Macbeth on hearing of his wife's death strike us as if, given the sequence of events, these words were automatically released by the last event in the series. The artistic "inevitability" lies in this complete adequacy of the external to the emotion; and this is precisely what is deficient in *Hamlet*. Hamlet (the man) is dominated by an emotion which is inexpressible, because it is in *excess* of the facts as they appear. (1950, 124–125)

This observation may be extended. The artist is obligated to pres-ent us with objective correlatives of particular emotions; that is the artist's vocation. But all of us may participate in this work. Let us say, for example, that you are daydreaming, and you find yourself in the presence of an imagined scene from your own history. You are driving the first car you ever owned, or you are back in your third-grade classroom. Such images will inevitably carry with them some of the emotional atmosphere that permeated that moment in your past. You not only see, but feel. Thus any spontaneously generated image—whether originated in memory or dream or discovered as an accidental fragment of the outside world—has the potential of being an objective correlative of some emotion, some complex, already established in our unconscious. Proust's madeleine is but the most famous example.

Eliot says, "The only way of expressing emotion in the form of art is by finding an objective correlative; ..." *Finding!* We expect this of artists but not of ourselves. Our example of the previous chapter, poor, dysthymic Prufrock, is pitiable because, even though he has seen the mermaids, he has given up seeking. The way out, for him, would be not just to see the mermaids but to engage with them. "I do not think that they will sing to me...." Perhaps not. But he might ask them to. He has to work on himself, or get help, to enable him to risk such asking. And there is hope: at the beginning of the poem, he has asked us to come along with him. He has approached a stranger. It is a start. When a patient shows up for the first session of psychoanalysis, that is already hopeful. When a person takes up reading, once again, books about a long-neglected interest, that is hopeful. Again: the operative word is *finding*. To find, one must begin to look. (The photographer Walker Evans knew an art teacher who was fond of saying, "Looking is much harder than it looks." True, but the point is to try.)

Here is a case history about looking. I present it as a case history because at this point I want to preserve the clinical distance that characterizes such writeups. I will change this stance later on.

L. is the second of four children born to a father who was well on his way to worldly success and his socially prominent wife. L. is a year younger than her older sister. The other two children (a boy and then a girl) were born seven and nine years later so that, in effect, there were two separate sets of children. L.'s infancy and early childhood were spent in a large Midwestern city, until the family moved to an affluent suburb. Father continued his rise in the business, civic, philanthropic and social life of the city, whereas the mother was somewhat insecure but a capable person who did participate in the social world. Some of her insecurity stemmed from the fact that she had not gone to college, whereas her husband was an Ivy League graduate. And she had a younger sister who was prettier, easier in the world, and who married several years before she did. Mother's insecurity mattered, but what was crucial was that L. was born extremely near-sighted. She could only see things that were nearly touching her; the rest of the world consisted of blurry, sometimes moving forms, which spoke but only occasionally touched her and then disappeared again into the mists. L.'s visual handicap was not recognized until she was three years old; she was then given strong glasses and did eye exercises for a few years, and she attended a public school which offered classes for the "partially sighted." She changed to private schools, got contact lenses, and did well enough. Her parents took her on a trip to Europe and, more importantly, to the theater. Musical comedy, especially, was wonderful for her. The theater was more real, more human, and more valuable than formal schooling. She graduated from a small liberal arts college and went on to study and practice interior design, and then photography—remarkable choices for a person with a history of visual impairment.

Not being able to see what is "out there," as an infant and a small child, is isolating in two ways. Obviously the child cannot know what is happening in the world except by interpreting sounds and language. But in L.'s case, there was another dimension. Her mother had little physical contact with her; she told L., years later, that she hardly ever picked her up when she was a baby. It was her more maternal father who usually administered eye drops. So, to the unnatural distance that her mother's reserved ways created, there was added this: *L. could not see whether she was being responded to or not.* Every researcher who has studied mother/infant interaction (for example, Winnicott, Bowlby, Stern, Bruner, and many others) makes a central point of the natural mirroring that must occur between mother and infant. One smiles, and the other smiles. One looks surprised, and the other responds to that expression. These exchanges are vital evidence for the baby that it can have an effect on another person.

We are dealing here with Waller's first wish: response. What does it mean not to know if one is being responded to? It means, I think, that very early on, such a child has to wonder, *Do I exist?* In L.'s case her profound nearsightedness is eventually diagnosed, glasses are provided, and the early (literally existential) sense of a void is gradually mitigated. The question, horrible as it is, sinks, repressed, into the unconscious, and is covered over by the natural strivings of ego in the world. Nevertheless, the question will lurk in the dark.

And it will be brought nearer to the surface over the years by a question L.'s father persistently asked her, in varied contexts: "Who do you think *you* are?" Probably he was not always completely serious, but he was serious enough of the time to make the question resonate with the deeper problem of existence.

It is reasonable to understand L., as she comes into adulthood, as a person who had a rich life, had satisfactory relationships with other people, had work that mattered to her, but who was also on psychological thin ice. I mean that image almost literally: the threat of falling through, to the depth of the waters of nonexistence, is always there. Then, in her early thirties, forces came together for her to undertake the photography for a book celebrating the American writer Willa Cather. It began when her father invited her to travel to Cather's Nebraska hometown, Red Cloud, and its surrounding prairie. Photographs she made there were in her first exhibit. Then, in the *Death Comes for the Archbishop* country of New Mexico, she recalled information from her father about a book being planned, and she contacted the University of Nebraska Press, which responded readily to the quality of her work as well as to the fact that she could manage the necessary travel. Cather herself had graduated from the University of Nebraska, where she had been in a Shakespeare class with L.'s grandmother. L.'s work involved a deep immersion in Cather's writing and travel to the settings of Cather's life and work: Virginia, Nebraska, Chicago, New York City, New Hampshire, New Mexico, Quebec; and, later, England, France, and Grand Manan Island. From a background of impaired vision and her tenuous connection to the outside world, L. responded openly to the physical world of light, landscape, and the suggestiveness of detail. Cather makes the great plains, and the New Mexico desert, into objective correlatives of the emotional states of her characters. L. strove to meet up with Cather's texts, and the freer she became in responding to particular moments in them and in Cather's settings, the better her photographs were. These were her "findings": photographs that went into the book, and many exhibits. L. used slides of her work to present her sense of Cather's places, life, the writing itself, and her own sense of journey that L. felt was basic for Cather—and herself, too. For L., Cather was both guide and companion, expressing the dark and the light. *Death Comes for the Archbishop,* for instance, weaves both murder and transcendence into ordinary daily life. Ántonia in *My Ántonia*, Paul in *Paul's Case*, Alexandra in *O Pioneers*—these and so many of Cather's characters live close to dark events, while at the same time there is the beauty of the landscape, and of the soul. Working with Cather, L. was mirrored as she was mirroring, in her exceptional photographs, the shadow and sunlight in one of America's most moving writers.

This is an example of what I have termed *finding*. In the end, finding and mirroring are the same: "finding" is the experience of having one's inner situation mirrored by someone or something in the outside world. It requires openness, as we have observed. The sterile repetitiveness of habit and custom will prevail until something new and unexpected is noticed and then pursued.

With this principle in mind I return now to my own story. By 1976, my marriage had foundered on the rocks of my wife's alcoholism and my attempts to do everything—work, write, teach and take care of my two children (now fifteen and twelve). I was all right in the outer world, but inside I was anxious, guilty, and worn out. The world I had known and grown up in and depended upon—the world of form—was of no use. I worked on anyway. I invented a course called "The Rhetoric of Photography," in which I applied principles of persuasion (Aristotle) to photographs, and invited students to do the same. Because I took my students to the Art Institute of Chicago's photography department so they could look at original prints, I got to know the photography curator, David Travis, and his then associate, Miles Barth, and they invited me to a photography opening in mid-December of 1976. I went, and was introduced to a photographer named Lucia Woods: the "L." of the case history just presented. As it happened, I had seen her photographs in a show the Art Institute gave her work two years before, and I remembered that many of them had to do with Willa Cather, whose writing I also knew something of. We had an immediate set of connections: photography, Cather, and—we both felt, immediately—something

"L," 1976

more. I was also instantly undone by her resemblance to S., in look (compare photograph of "S." p. 109), in voice, in manner, and in what I felt as an exciting calm.

Something of the initial wonderment that came over me at Oxford those many years ago returned in the moment Lucia and I met. And, remembering Lucia's photographs from her Art Institute show, I realized how clearly they had stayed with me. They were not just "about" Cather and her writings; they probed deeper. They were objective correlatives in themselves: the Nebraska prairie seen as both a rich and a brutal home for Ántonia and Alexandra and Cather's other pioneer figures; New Mexico, with its exotic contrasts of sky and monotonous desert seen as spiritual settings; remote Quebec had its quality of home, and so on.

As Lucia and I got to know one another, it became evident that we shared the sense of being on a quest. I carried on my quest indirectly, through poetry and teaching. Lucia's was direct, not only through photography but also through therapy and analysis, and the keeping of a journal—the Progoff Intensive Journal—that records inner flux, images, and characters. Within two years we married. Soon after, I wrote, in an article about photography, that "all of us, no matter when or where, arrange ourselves and our possessions in ways bordering on the magical: ways intended to project our inner ideas of order out into the otherwise neutral universe of inanimate things. Thus do we maintain... our sense of self" (1982, 167–168). That was what Lucia was doing, and not only in her photographic work. Since we married, she has shaped my world: making two homes into uniquely personal spaces that are serene, original, and, for me, always receptive; spaces that allow for thought and feeling to grow, unhindered by form or custom, or by shoulds and oughts. And recently she has begun to make small changes in my Old Black Point house, changes that reflect our pleasure in art and objects and move it subtly forward in time without losing the spirit of my parents and grandparents. Now there is an amusing posterlike painting of George Washington in the hallway, and portraits of gloomy ancestors in the dining room have been replaced by unusual botanical prints in which immense seeded fruits hover over tiny towns and cities.

Above all we share photography. Lucia sees photography as a dance. The photographer moves around her subject, and that motion "causes" motion in the subject as spatial relationships and angles of light change. This is like the relationship between a pair of dancers, each one affecting the other, each one reacting to the other. Thus any subject of a photograph is as active as the photographer. The idea that the photographer "takes" or "makes" the photograph is undermined. The subject and the photographer create the photograph together. Each mirrors the other. Lucia's photographs are of their subjects and beyond them at the same time. In her work she embodies, carries out, the very *finding* that challenges consciousness itself with a larger vision.

What we unconsciously shared when we met is now, twenty-eight years later, apparent to us. We were both searching, trying to verify the reality of our own being. She, because that reality had been undermined for so long by the troubling, painful fact of not being seen; I, because my parents could not see me without unconsciously reviving the fear of death that had gripped them at my birth, and also because I had for so long compromised my own reality by living in a world ordered by form and custom. Lucia and I met at the precise moment in our lives when, together, we could and did enter an unknown world—unknown because it would be a new way of being for both of us. Rather than looking for, or trying to live within, a permanent "answer," we had come to a place where the task of *finding* was what we were both about. As I have said, in order to find, one must seek.

Let us see where this leads. The following principles operate, in this stage of life—if we are open enough:

1) The world is full of objective correlatives; that is, the outer world serendipitously mirrors our inner landscape, our particular constellations of archetypal images.
2) We must be open, therefore, to the potency of particular images for ourselves;

3) We must allow those particular images to take over our conscious minds, at least from time to time, in order to gain a balance between the conscious and the unconscious domains. In other words, we must suffer the relativization of our own ego. Here, "suffer" means "allow," but there will be pain and loss, too. Ego wants to stay in control.

"Truths that wake / To perish never" are at once perceived by the ego—everything is—and then are immediately undermined by it because they are larger, numinous, and more constant than ego. Even so, they are the object of the quest. They produce an acceptance of who we are and an importunate urge to move on, to keep on finding. Tennyson's *Ulysses* is once again our example:

> Though much is taken, much abides; and though
> We are not now that strength which in old days
> Moved earth and heaven; that which we are, we are;
> One equal temper of heroic hearts,
> Made weak by time and fate, but strong in will
> To strive, to seek, to find, and not to yield. (1968, 843)

Lucia and I knew, from the moment we met, that there was something common to both of us. At first we had no idea what. Our life together has been an exploration of our common ground. Obviously, we do not expect to finish this quest in our lifetimes. The ego of early adulthood believes in final answers; time undermines this illusion. Waller's "new experience" (for us in theater, literature, art, our own objects and living spaces, photography, travel, other people) and the history of relatives and children, whether positive or painful, has continued. *New experience has become more secure than security.* It keeps reminding us of the infinite variety of life itself. The larger structures we intuited that we shared have been there for us. They are there for everyone: the symbolic ground is common property. The archetypes are universal. Plato, in the *Phaedo,* wrote of our soul having had a prior existence among the eternal, pure Forms, an existence

that our being born into this world causes us to forget. That image is
Wordsworth's source:

> Our birth is but a sleep and a forgetting:
> The Soul that rises with us, our life's Star,
> Hath had elsewhere its setting,
> And cometh from afar:
> Not in entire forgetfulness,
> And not in utter nakedness,
> But trailing clouds of glory do we come .... (1948, 232)

When we find evidence of those "clouds of glory" our sense of
ourselves is changed, however slightly, forever. Willa Cather gives
these words to her archbishop:

> The Miracles of the Church seem to me to rest not so much
> upon faces or voices or healing power coming suddenly near to
> us from afar off, but upon our perceptions being made finer, so
> that for a moment our eyes can see and our ears can hear what
> is there about us always. (1971, 50)

The task, the challenge, and the joy is to be open to surprise. Not
overwhelming or rapturous or awful surprise; rather, the surprises
contained in ordinary experience: "There's a certain slant of light,"
Emily Dickinson noticed, and a rumination began. For her, it ended
in a poem:

> There's a certain Slant of light,
> Winter Afternoons—
> That oppresses, like the heft
> Of Cathedral Tunes—
>
> Heavenly Hurt, it gives us—
> We can find no scar,
> But internal difference,
> Where the Meanings, are—
> None may teach it—Any—
> 'Til the Seal Despair—

An imperial affliction
Sent us of the Air—

When it comes, the Landscape listens—
Shadows—hold their breath—
When it goes, 'tis like the Distance
On the look of Death—   (1976, 328)

We are not poets. But the way the light falls on some bit of our world can begin a memory, a sense of the way things were. Or a new vision may begin to form in us. The task, and the victory, of this time of life, is to seek such things. Seeking sometimes becomes finding. The patterns are there. That is why "seeking itself is the way." We seek "Internal difference, Where the Meanings, are" and we find those meanings when our lives are caught and brought back to us by "what is there about us always."

CHAPTER 7

OLD AGE AS OPENNESS
PRIMAL SYMPATHY

Here, once again, is the *Intimations* Ode, nearing its conclusion. Wordsworth is done with recollections. He writes now of the future, a future of peaceful, constructive contemplation of a timeless "primal sympathy" that—like the archetypes—has always existed and will go on forever:

> Though nothing can bring back the hour
> Of splendor in the grass, of glory in the flower;
> We will grieve not, rather find
> Strength in what remains behind;
> In the primal sympathy
> Which having been must ever be;
> In the soothing thoughts that spring
> Out of human suffering;
> In the faith that looks through death,
> In years that bring the philosophic mind.
>
> (1948, 234)

It is a vision of old age that gives a new and inspiring meaning to "going on being," Winnicott's phrase for the essential experience of infancy. One vision of old age, then, is staying in the world as it is, and viewing it with "the philosophic mind" while at the same time going on being.

Now, compare that conception—this wish, if you will—with the wish contained in this poem by W. B. Yeats. (In the first line, the country is Yeats' Ireland.)

Sailing to Byzantium

I

That is no country for old men. The young
In one another's arms, birds in the trees
—Those dying generations—at their song,
The salmon-falls, the mackerel-crowded seas,
Fish, flesh, or fowl, commend all summer long
Whatever is begotten, born, and dies.
Caught in that sensual music all neglect
Monuments of unageing intellect.

II

An aged man is but a paltry thing,
A tattered coat upon a stick, unless
Soul clap its hands and sing, and louder sing
For every tatter in its mortal dress,
Nor is there singing school but studying
Monuments of its own magnificence;
And therefore I have sailed the seas and come
To the holy city of Byzantium.

III

O sages standing in God's holy fire
As in the gold mosaic of a wall,
Come from the holy fire, perne in a gyre,
And be the singing-masters of my soul.
Consume my heart away; sick with desire
And fastened to a dying animal
It knows not what it is; and gather me
Into the artifice of eternity.

IV

Once out of nature I shall never take
My bodily form from any natural thing,
But such a form as Grecian goldsmiths make
Of hammered gold and gold enamelling

To keep a drowsy Emperor awake;
Or set upon a golden bough to sing
To lords and ladies of Byzantium
Of what is past, or passing, or to come.

(1989, 193–194)

Where Wordsworth imagines going on being, Yeats imagines being transformed out of nature entirely. This is not death. Rather, he imagines a transformation from mortal flesh into immortal *art*, a golden bird. We have already seen how art stays constant in the face of our own ageing: Hamlet will always be Hamlet, will always question his world; Prufrock will always be intimidated by his own existence. But Wordsworth and Yeats propose two ways of thinking about old age: either we go on being, but with a more philosophic mind, or we hope to be transformed. Yeats posits being "out of nature," which means out of clock time, out of life itself as we know it. Any reader will readily understand and probably agree with Yeats's idea of old age as the state of being "fastened to a dying animal." Wishing to be transformed into a golden bird, though, is less familiar, even if it can see into the future and sing to lords and ladies. Neither poet contemplates the ordinary tribulations of ageing. Let us look more closely at these two visions.

Once again, I cite that sublime moment in *King Lear* when he, imprisoned with Cordelia and reconciled with her at last, imagines going on being. (He is able to do this because he has finally given up his false conflation of adulthood with kingship.)

Lear (to Cordelia): . . . Come, let's away to prison.
We two alone will sing like birds i'th' cage.
When thou dost ask me blessing, I'll kneel down
And ask of thee forgiveness; so we'll live,
And pray, and sing, and tell old tales, and laugh
At gilded butterflies, and hear poor rogues
Talk of court news, and we'll talk with them too—
Who loses and who wins, who's in, who's out,
And take upon 's the mystery of things

> As if we were God's spies; and we'll wear out
> In a walled prison packs and sects of great ones
> That ebb and flow by the moon.

Edmund (to soldiers): Take them away.

(1986, V, 3)

They will be taken, of course, to their deaths. But in this one moment of transcendent vision, the aged king foresees Wordsworth's wish for the "years that bring the philosophic mind." And more than that: they will be "God's spies." That will enable them to take upon themselves "the mystery of things." *King Lear* is a tragedy because Cordelia and her father die at the very moment when this hope has become, at last, absolutely vivid and real. But what if they had miraculously survived? What if the king had lived with the knowledge of the mystery of things? Would he go on being? Or would he be transformed?

It is purely wonderful that we do not have to imagine this happiest of outcomes: Shakespeare has given us King Lear and Cordelia, surviving. They are Prospero and his daughter, Miranda, in *The Tempest*. Prospero *has* taken on the mystery of things, and uses that knowledge. Miranda lives to discover humanity itself, most ecstatically in the form of Ferdinand, her husband-to-be.

Compare Prospero with King Lear. King Lear lived his life involved—too involved—with the politics of kingship itself. He never reflected, never introspectively considered his life's journey and his own humanity, until it was too late. Prospero is just the opposite. By way of plot summary: he lost his dukedom because he was so wrapped up in his esoteric studies that he failed to see his own brother plotting against him, plotting to usurp the political power inherent in the dukedom of Milan. Then, cast away on a remote island with his young daughter, Prospero continues to study, turning his knowledge to practical use, and assuming control of the island by subjugating its several supernatural inhabitants. Empowered by this initial victory, he waits until the courtiers of Milan sail within range, whereupon he creates a magical tempest that brings them ashore on his tiny dukedom. King Lear's control is political, and he is forced to give it up, which leads to the open moment we have seen, and then to death. Prospero's control is based on knowledge, on his staff and his book. It is control he can, and will, give up:

> But this rough magic
> I here abjure. And when I have required
> Some heavenly music—which even now I do—
> To work mine end upon their senses that
> This airy charm is for, I'll break my staff,
> Bury it certain fathoms in the earth,
> And deeper than did any plummet sound
> I'll drown my book (1986, IV, 1, lines 50–57)

Unlike the king, Prospero is in control both when he has power and when he does not. Not that it is complete control. Ariel, the positive aspect of Prospero's power, works to be free of Prospero's authority. And Caliban, the dark side of that same power, remains recalcitrant until the very end, when he says, I think somewhat unpersuasively, "... I'll be wise hereafter, / And seek for grace." Prospero's triumph is complete: Miranda will marry Ferdinand, the plotters will be foiled, the good rewarded, and Prospero will be restored to his rightful dukedom.

To what, then, does Prospero's knowledge lead? Does Wordsworth's "philosophic mind" imply Prosperonian control? I do not think so. What such knowledge leads to is a sense of the connection between psychic order and worldly order: "We'll be God's spies, and take upon 's the mystery of things." Or, recall Herakles' vision, even in his agony: "*SPLENDOUR! IT ALL COHERES!*" Prospero himself famously concludes that everything is ephemeral.

> These our actors,
> As I foretold you, were all spirits, and
> Are melted into air, into thin air;
> And, like the baseless fabric of this vision,

> The cloud-capped towers, the gorgeous palaces,
> The solemn temples, the great globe itself,
> Yea, all which it inherit, shall dissolve;
> And, like this insubstantial pageant faded,
> Leave not a wrack behind. We are such stuff
> As dreams are made on, and our little life
> Is rounded with a sleep. (1986, IV, 1)

Much has been made of these words. For years I felt they represented all that might be said of eschatology. But consider: a "wrack" is a small cloud. Not even such a wisp will be left. King Lear saw far greater possibilities before him; and he, like Prospero, was with his child, always an embodiment of the future. Prospero's speech is moving, and has the ring of profundity, but it skips over the one idea that could lead us to a better understanding of what we are: *We are such stuff as dreams are made on.* Exactly. Dreams come from somewhere; they are not random, or casually created. They have structure and purpose and meaning. As we have seen, the dreamer-in-the-dream, the dream ego, is always open to new experience. For this reason the dream ego is the eternal child. Thus, even in old age, the child is present, every night, and any time we are open to it.

Here is Willa Cather's archbishop. His life is coming to a close, and yet:

In New Mexico he always awoke a young man; not until he rose and began to shave did he realize he was growing older. His first consciousness was a sense of the light dry wind blowing in through the windows, with a fragrance of hot sun and sage-brush and sweet clover; a wind that made one's body feel light and one's heart cry "to-day, to-day," like a child's.

Beautiful surroundings, the society of learned men, the charm of noble women, the graces of art, could not make up for him the loss of those light-hearted mornings of the desert, for the wind that made one a boy again. He had noticed that this peculiar quality in the air of new countries vanished after they were tamed by man and were made to bear harvests. Parts of Texas and Kansas that he had first known as open range had since been made into rich farming districts, and the air had quite lost that lightness, that dry aromatic odour. The moisture of plowed land, the heaviness of labour and growth and grain-bearing, utterly destroyed it; one could breathe that only on the bright edge of the world, on the great grass plains or the sage-brush desert.

That air would disappear from the whole earth in time, perhaps; but long after his day. He did not know just when it had become so necessary to him, but he had come back to die in exile for the sake of it. Something soft and wild and free, something that whispered to the ear on the pillow, lightened the heart, softly, softly picked the lock, slid the bolts, and released the prisoned spirit of man into the wind, into the blue and gold, into the morning, into the morning! (1971, 275–276)

This is not dissolution, not something melted into thin air, not "the baseless fabric of this vision." In contrast to Prospero's sense of things, this is not the end; it is the opposite. It is the *morning*.

Old age, I believe, is the morning. Not of life itself, obviously, but the beginning of an idea of wholeness. Note "beginning." That is the morning aspect of this vision. It is no wonder that elderly people remember best those events which happened long ago; they are drawn to beginnings, just as the archbishop is drawn to the primordial earth. That deep past is always there, as are the archetypes that underlie it. Old age is for the exploration of what is eternal in each present moment.

There is another image in the archbishop's rumination: the spirit of man, he imagines, is released "into the wind, into the blue and gold," as well as into the morning; indeed blue and gold are morning colors. But if wind is ephemeral, blue and gold *may* be constants. The sky is always blue above the clouds. Gold is unchanging, the essence of purity, and an embodiment of the sun, the sun trapped in the earth, then found and treasured. Remember now the golden bird set upon a golden bough. It is the artifice of eternity, which brings us, finally, to final things.

Yeats's poem portrays a narrator who sees no hope "unless / Soul clap its hands and sing, and louder sing / For every tatter in its mortal dress." To celebrate one's own tatters is to celebrate things as they are, and this, in turn, means being able to see things as they are. Such seeing is not easy. Prufrock can't do it. Neither can Hamlet, until near the end. King Lear is especially deceived. We are all deceived, to the extent that we live within a prison of complexes, or subservient to the demands of an impersonal collective or a corrosive relationship. Yeats celebrates "every tatter," every flaw, every fault; he sings in celebration of what is actually there. The poem says of such singing, "Nor is there singing school but studying / Monuments of its own magnificence." In other words, the place—the only place—to learn to celebrate so exuberantly is the singing school. What sort of a school is it? Its curriculum, I suggest, is entirely training in noticing: how to be aware of as much as possible for as long as possible, everywhere and at all times. In *Our Town,* Wilder's heroine, Emily, dies in childbirth but is allowed to return to earth for one day. She returns knowing she will never again be alive on earth. This makes her notice *everything* doubly: as it was, and as it is for her now, seen from death's domain. She smells the breakfast coffee and at the same time knows she will never experience this—or any earthly thing else—again. The world experienced this way is too much for her to bear. As she is returning to the domain of the dead, she asks the almost omniscient Stage Manager, in some desperation, whether anyone experiences the world as she has just done. He tells her that maybe the saints and poets do, some.

Saints and poets. We have looked, throughout, at poetry, and we have seen it reflect a deep sense of being with one's self and being in the world. Most of us are not poets or artists. But poets and artists give us the chance to experience intensity, albeit vicariously. They have been to singing school. They have found ways to celebrate the monuments of their own souls' magnificence—or despair, or beauty, or surprise. Prufrock heard the mermaids because Eliot knew he himself could. Hamlet knew, before he died, that the world had been set right, and that he was forgiven. Both Eliot and Shakespeare were able to celebrate the tatters of their mortality.

Yeats, though, goes on from this: he asks that the Byzantine saints emerge from the mosaics and become the singing-masters (that image again) of his soul. If they do, he hopes they will consume his heart away, will strip him of his animal, time-limited mortality, and gather him into "the artifice of eternity."

Note carefully: not eternity, but the *artifice* of eternity. An artifice is enough. Artifice; art. Art will do. Art is sufficient: A bird out of nature, a golden bird, a work of art, a bird that is able to sing of past, present, and future. Precisely because it is out of nature, art is beyond time, beyond the threshold of mortality. Looking back, as in old age we can, it is possible to see our history as having been shaped by eternal forms, the archetypes. We have been partly responsible for the shaping, but we have also been shaped. In that sense we are, and always have been, works of art.

Once again:

> Our birth is but a sleep and a forgetting:
> The Soul that rises with us, our life's Star,
> Hath had elsewhere its setting,
> And cometh from afar:
> Not in entire forgetfulness,
> And not in utter nakedness,
> But trailing clouds of glory do we come
> From God, who is our home. (1948, 232)

The golden bird Yeats wishes to become has always been there, and will always be. Gold endures. The privilege of age is to know this, to know that there is an eternal pattern within which we find our own individual ways and which, when we see that pattern for ourselves, gives meaning to all experience. With such a vision, the question of whether going on being is to be desired, or whether being transformed out of nature is to be desired, is no longer a concern.

Each is equally valuable. Opposite though they are, they become one another, in the end. To be aware of the archetypal ground is to live where the particulars of our story and the eternal foundation of that story become inseparable. There can be no time without timelessness. Wordsworth asked,

> Whither is fled the visionary gleam?
> Where is it now, the glory and the dream? (1948, 232)

In time, he found his answer: the visionary gleam, the glory, and the dream are always with us:

> Thanks to the human heart by which we live,
> Thanks to its tenderness, its joys, and fears,
> To me the meanest flower that blows can give
> Thoughts that do often lie too deep for tears. (1948, 234)

The room in which I am writing has photographs (some of which are in this book) of the Old Black Point shoreline on its walls—photographs I have made over many years. Here is the grape arbor at the end of the terrace, with the sun behind it setting into the Long Island Sound. In another (page 34), sunlight sparkles on that water, making starlike bits of brilliance. Or (page 36), small, round rocks shine as the tide comes in over them. Soon I will be on that shore once again. I will sit on the terrace and watch the sunset as I have for so many summers, and I will hear again the cry of terns and gulls. To be on the shore is to be between the known land and the unknown water. The land is permanent, the sea is always in flux, always moving, or moved by the winds:

> The salt is on the briar rose,
> The fog is in the fir trees.
> > The sea howl
> And the sea yelp, are different voices
> Often together heard: the whine in the rigging,
> The menace and caress of wave that breaks on water,
> The distant rote in the granite teeth,
> And the wailing warning from the approaching headland

Are all sea voices, and the heaving groaner
Rounded homewards, and the seagull:
And under the oppression of the silent fog
The tolling bell
Measures time not our time, rung by the unhurried
Ground swell, a time
Older than the time of chronometers....

(1944, 21–22)

Thus T. S. Eliot, remembering a similar shore from his own early life. All of us have our own shoreline, our own place where one state of being turns into its opposite: known to unknown. In old age we stand on this shore. My grandmother, who spent so many summers in this house that is now mine, was a person I found endlessly amusing. She had her ways. Every summer, every time we went anywhere in the car, as we drove out of our driveway, she would cry, "Off we go in a cloud of dust! Everything looks familiar." When I was a child I found this funny, but incomprehensible. There was never any cloud of dust, and of course everything always looked familiar. But what she said, I now see, was profoundly true, whether she thought of that way or not. There is the mystery: we will go off in a cloud of dust. But the archetypal ground, because it has always been there, will be familiar. The world forever keeps us mindful of that familiarity with its patterns: its seasons and tides, its light and darkness. In "East Coker," Eliot, too, reminds us that old age is the time for discovering what is always there in "every moment":

> Home is where one starts from. As we grow older
> The world becomes stranger, the pattern more complicated
> Of dead and living. Not the intense moment
> Isolated, with no before and after,
> But a lifetime burning in every moment
> And not the lifetime of one man only
> But of old stones that cannot be deciphered.
> There is a time for the evening under starlight,
> A time for the evening under lamplight
> (The evening with the photograph album).
> Love is most nearly itself
> When here and now cease to matter.
> Old men ought to be explorers
> Here or there does not matter.
> We must be still and still moving
> Into another intensity
> For a further union, a deeper communion

Through the dark cold and the empty desolation,
The wave cry, the wind cry, the vast waters
Of the petrel and the porpoise. In my end is my beginning.

(1944, 17)

REFERENCES

Anobile, R.J. 1971. *Why a Duck?* New York: Darien House Inc.

Auden, W. H. 1962. *The Dyer's Hand.* New York: Random House.

Beckett, Samuel. 1976. *I Can't Go On, I'll Go On: A Samuel Beckett Reader,* edited by Richard W. Seaver. New York: Grove Press.

Bloom, Harold. 2003. *Hamlet: Poem Unlimited.* New York: Riverhead Books.

Bowlby, John. 1969. *Attachment.* New York: Basic Books.

Breasted, James Henry. [1912] 1972. *Development of Religion and Thought in Ancient Egypt.* Philadelphia: University of Pennsylvania Press.

————. 1912. *A History of Egypt.* New York: Charles Scribner's Sons.

Cather, Willa. 1971. *Death Comes for the Archbishop.* New York: Vintage Books.

Crain, William C. 1985. *Theories of Development: Concepts and Applications,* 2nd ed., Englewood Cliffs, NJ: Prentice-Hall.

Cummings, E. E. 1954. *Poems, 1923–1954.* New York: Harcourt, Brace.

Damasio, Antonio. 1999. *The Feeling of What Happens.* New York: Harcourt, Inc.

Dickinson, Emily. 1976. "There's a certain Slant of light." In *The New Oxford Book of American Verse,* edited by Richard Ellmann. New York: Oxford University Press.

Edinger, Edward. 1972. *Ego and Archetype.* New York: Pelican Books.

Eliot, T. S. 1936. *Collected Poems, 1909–1935.* New York: Harcourt, Brace and Company.

————. 1939. *The Family Reunion.* New York: Harcourt, Brace.

————. 1943. *Four Quartets.* New York: Harcourt, Brace.

————. 1950. "Tradition and the Individual Talent," in *The Sacred Wood.* London: Faber and Faber.

————. 1975. *Selected Prose of T.S. Eliot,* edited by Frank Kermode. New York: Farrar, Straus and Giroux.

Ferlinghetti, Lawrence. 1958. *A Coney Island of the Mind.* New York: New Directions.

Forman, Werner and Stephen Quirke. 1996. *Hieroglyphics and the Afterlife in Ancient Egypt.* Norman: University of Oklahoma Press.

Frankel, Richard. 1998. *The Adolescent Psyche: Jungian and Winnicottian Perspectives.* London: Routledge.

Frost, Robert. 1976. "Desert Places." In *The New Oxford Book of American Verse,* edited by Richard Ellmann. New York: Oxford University Press.

Galassi, Peter. 2000. *Walker Evans and Company.* New York: Museum of Modern Art.

Gordon, Lyndall. 1998. *T.S. Eliot: An Imperfect Life.* New York: W.W. Norton.

Hall, Donald, ed. 1957. *New Poets of England and America.* Cleveland: Meridian Books.

Hart, Mickey. 1990. *Drumming at the Edge of Magic,* with Jay Stevens. New York: HarperSanFrancisco.

Hogensen, George. 2001. "The Baldwin Effect: A Neglected Influence on C. G. Jung's Evolutionary Thinking," *Journal of Analytical Psychology,* 46 (4): 591–612.

Jaynes, Julian. 1976. *The Origin of Consciousness in the Breakdown of the Bicameral Mind.* Boston: Houghton Mifflin.

Jung, C. G. 1963. *Memories, Dreams, Reflections.* New York: Pantheon Books.

———. 1971. *Psychological Types. Collected Works* vol. 6. Princeton, NJ: Princeton University Press.

———. 1970. *Freud and Psychoanalysis. Collected Works* vol. 4. Princeton, NJ: Princeton University Press.

———. 1970. *Letters,* edited by Gerhard Adler and Aniela Jaffe. Princeton, NJ: Princeton University Press.

———. 1966. *The Practice of Psychotherapy. Collected Works* vol. 16. Princeton, NJ: Princeton University Press.

———. 1954. *The Development of Personality. Collected Works* vol. 17. Princeton, NJ: Princeton University Press.

Knox, Jean. 2003. *Archetype, Attachment, Analysis.* Hove, England: Brunner-Routledge.

Kohut, Heinz. 1985. *Self Psychology and the Humanities.* New York: W. W. Norton.

Lehner, Mark. 1997. *The Complete Pyramids.* London: Thames and Hudson.

Lindley, Daniel. 1970. "Rhetorical Analysis of Teaching Process in Selected English Classes." *Dissertation Abstracts International* 31, 09-A, 4601.

———. 1982. "Walker Evans, Rhetoric, and Photography." In *Reading Into Photography,* edited by Thomas F. Barrow, Shelley Armitage, and William E. Tydeman. Albuquerque: New Mexico University Press.

McLuhan, Marshall. 1965. *Understanding Media.* New York: McGraw-Hill.

Meltzer, Donald, and M. H. Williams. 1988. *The Apprehension of Beauty.* Old Ballechin, Strath Tay, Scotland: Clunie Press.

Moffett, James. 1988. *Storm in the Mountains*. Carbondale: Southern Illinois University Press.

Mouton, A. 2004. "Messages from the Gods." *The Oriental Institute News and Notes*, 180, 1–4.

Neumann, Erich. 1970. *The Origins and History of Consciousness*. Princeton, NJ: Princeton University Press.

Nightingale, Florence. 1987. *Letters from Egypt: A Journey on the Nile*, edited by A. Sattin. New York: Weidenfeld and Nicholson.

Perry, John Weir. 1966. *Lord of the Four Quarters: Myths of the Royal Father*. New York: George Braziller.

Pope, Alexander. 1969. "Essay on Man." In *Poetry and Prose of Alexander Pope*, edited by Aubrey Williams. Boston: Houghton Mifflin.

Pound, Ezra. 2003. *Poems and Translations*. New York: The Library of America.

Progoff, Ira. 1975. *At a Journal Workshop: The Basic Text and Guide for Using the Intensive Journal*. New York: Dialogue House Library.

Reed, Bika. 1978. *Rebel in the Soul*. New York: Inner Traditions International.

Samuels, Andrew, and Fred Plaut. 1986. *A Critical Dictionary of Jungian Analysis*. London and New York: Routledge and Kegan Paul.

Sexton, Anne. 1974. *The Death Notebooks*. Boston: Houghton Mifflin.

Shakespeare, William. 1986. *The Complete Plays*, edited by Stanley Wells and Gary Taylor. Oxford: Clarendon Press. All citations from Shakespeare are from this edition.

Singer, June. 1994. *Boundaries of the Soul*. New York: Anchor Books.

Stein, Murray. 1998. *Jung's Map of the Soul*. Chicago: Open Court Press.

Stern, Daniel. 1985. *The Interpersonal World of the Infant*. New York: Basic Books.

Szpakowska, Kasia. 2003. *Behind Closed Eyes: Dreams and Nightmares in Ancient Egypt*. Swansea: Classical Press of Wales.

Teeter, Emily. 1997. *The Presentation of Maat*. Chicago: University of Chicago Press.

Tennyson, Alfred. 1968. "Ulysses." In *The Norton Anthology of English Literature*, vol. 2, edited by M. L. Abrams et al. New York: W. W. Norton.

Thomas, Dylan. 1953. *The Collected Poems of Dylan Thomas*. New York: New Directions.

Tolman, Edward Chace. 1951. *Collected Papers in Psychology*. Berkeley and Los Angeles: University of California Press.

Turner, Victor W. 1967. *The Forest of Symbols: Aspects of Ndembu Ritual*. Ithaca, NY: Cornell University Press.

van Gennep, A. 1960. *The Rites of Passage.* Chicago: University of Chicago Press.

Vendler, Helen. 1997. *Poems, Poets, Poetry.* Boston: Bedford Books / St. Martin's Press.

Waller, Willard. 1933. *The Sociology of Teaching.* New York: Russell and Russell.

Whitmont, Edward. 1969. *The Symbolic Quest.* Princeton, NJ: Princeton University Press.

Winnicott, D. W. 1965. *The Maturational Process and the Facilitating Environment.* New York: International Universities Press, Inc.

———. 1975. *Through Paediatrics to Psycho-analysis.* New York: Basic Books, Inc.

Wordsworth, William. 1948. *Anthology of Romanticism*, edited by Ernest Birnbaum. New York: Ronald Press Company. All citations from Wordsworth are from this edition.

Yeats, W. B. 1989. *The Collected Works of W. B. Yeats.* vol 1, *The Poems.* edited by Richard J. Finneran. New York: Macmillan.

INDEX